Raised for His Glory

Fred DeRuvo

Raised for His Glory

Copyright © 2011 by Study-Grow-Know

All rights reserved. Written permission must be secured from the publisher to use or reproduce any part of this book, except brief quotations in critical reviews or articles.

Some material in this book has been previously published in *Anti-zionism's Vitriolic Allegations*, authored by Fred DeRuvo

Published in Scotts Valley, California, by Study-Grow-Know
www.studygrowknow.com • www.rightly-dividing.com

Unless noted, Scripture quotations are from the New American Standard Bible, Copyright ©1960, 1962, 1963, 1968, 1971, 1972, 1973, 1975, 1977, 1995 by The Lockman Foundation.

Cover design by Fred DeRuvo

All images unless otherwise noted were created by Fred DeRuvo

Woodcuts used herein are used with permission of Dover Publications

Cover Image by: © kaetana - Fotolia.com

Oneplace.com logo on back outside cover is a registered trademark of Oneplace.com

Edited by: Hannah Richards

Library of Congress Cataloging-in-Publication Data

DeRuvo, Fred, 1957 –

ISBN 0983700621
EAN-13 978-0983700623

1. Religion – Christian Theology - Apologetics

Contents

Foreword: 5
Chapter 1: For the Sake of His Name 7
Chapter 2: Resurrection of Israel 18
Chapter 3: Beyond the Valley of the Bones 30
Chapter 4: The Northern Invasion 35
Chapter 5: Gog Knows 47
Chapter 6: Gog Pays the Price 55
Chapter 7: The Aftermath 64
Chapter 8: God Desires Restoration 70
Chapter 9: Will Israel Rise Again? 74
Chapter 10: Attacks on Scripture 85
Chapter 11: The Spiritual Jew 116
Chapter 12: Replacement? 144
Chapter 13: God's Promises Will Prevail 168
Chapter 14: What About You? 177

"Therefore say to the house of Israel, 'Thus says the Lord GOD, "It is not for your sake, O house of Israel, that I am about to act, but for My holy name, which you have profaned among the nations where you went. I will vindicate the holiness of My great name which has been profaned among the nations, which you have profaned in their midst. Then the nations will know that I am the LORD," declares the Lord GOD, "when I prove Myself holy among you in their sight."

– Ezekiel 36:22-24 (NASB)

FOREWORD

Israel, oh *Israel*. What is happening with Israel? What *appears* to be occurring is exactly what God said would occur when He spoke through the prophet Ezekiel. What the world seems to be noticing is that Israel is a "terrorist" nation that simply wants to show unfavorable attitudes and demeanor toward the "Palestinians."

Should we accept the world's point of view or God's? It would appear that many more Christians today seem to be siding with the world. Could it be that they have simply become too tired of all the wars, skirmishes, and rumors of wars in the Middle East? Is it possible that many Christians today have turned their ear to theologians who believe that when Ezekiel is speaking *to* or *about* the nation of Israel or the Land of Israel, somehow he is actually speaking of the Church that would not be born for hundreds of years yet?

What does God's Word say about Israel, both the Land *and* the nation of Israel? Does God have a plan for Israel or not? When Israel once again became a nation in 1948, was it an accident or fulfillment of God's Word to and through Ezekiel?

This persistent belief that Israel should not have any place in the Middle East, or that Israel should kowtow to neighbors who bear nothing but ill will towards her, is a growing concern. On a larger scale, Israel is being hemmed in on all sides.

Yet tiny Israel, a virtual island among warmongering nations, has continued to exist against any and all odds. Whether it was the Six-Day War of 1967, the continued escalation in fighting, the full scale assault on Israel through illegal weapons smuggled into that country using tunnels under Israeli ground, or something else, Israel has not succumbed to the will of the growing majority of nations and people who have resolutely sided against her. Israel has continued to exist and has done so in the fact of tremendous odds.

Israel is a Land and a nation that God created. He specifically stated to Abraham that those who bless Israel would be blessed and those who curse Israel would be cursed (cf. Genesis 12, 15, and 17). That promise has never been rescinded, yet people act as if that has been the case.

Prime Minister Netanyahu recently addressed the United States Congress. During his speech, a woman interrupted him to condemn the acts of Israel. She – as an American and a Jew – believes that Israel has treated "Palestinians" wrongly and believed that she had a case when she stood up, waved her banner, and yelled, "*equal rights for Palestinians!*" before she was escorted from the chambers, assaulted, and arrested from her hospital bed.[1]

What people seem to fail to realize is that God's promise of blessing or cursing is *not* dependent upon how Israel treats anyone. God will deal with Israel, as He has done many times throughout Israel's history. It is not up to the people of this world to assign themselves the task of policing the Land or nation that God Himself created. God will deal with it. What authentic Christians are supposed to do is to continue to evangelize Jews of this world, just as we are to evangelize Gentiles of this world. Beyond this we are to support Israel for no other reason that God has said we should, and there is blessing in doing that.

What about Israel today? Is God done with her? Has He somehow transferred that promise to Abraham *from* Israel and *to* the Church? This book serves to answer that question.

Fred DeRuvo, July 2011

---

[1] http://www.cbsnews.com/8301-503544_162-20065711-503544.html (accessed 5/30/2011)

1

For the Sake of His Name

There is a good deal of talk today about peace in the Middle East. There is also a great deal of *acrimony* where Israel is concerned because of this alleged peace process. Insults and vitriol are routinely placed at the feet of Israel because of her alleged unwillingness to foster peace with the Arab nations that surround her, in spite of what she has constantly given.

I expect this talk from the world. I don't expect it from people who call themselves Christians, yet this is increasingly becoming more of the norm.

People do not realize how they contradict themselves. On one hand they say that Israel controls the foreign policy of the United States, while on the other hand, they say that "the Jews" control the media. On both counts, they are wrong.

Logically, if "the Jews" controlled the media, there would obviously be far less acrimony toward Israel than there is today. Instead, what do we have in the world? We have a tremendous sympathy toward Arabs and Muslims and the world's collective heart goes out particularly to the "Palestinians" within the Land of Israel. The world believes they have gotten a raw deal and the fault lies with Israel.

Yet, Israel – or at least "the Jews" – controls the media. If so, how could Israel have allowed the tide to turn against them? People who believe that "the Jews" control the media obviously also believe that certain editorials that allegedly reveal the deep, dark secrets of Israel's misbehavior have managed to squeak in under the noses of "the Jews" that control the media. Does this even seem logical?

Whether it's *The New York Times*, *The Washington Post*, or some other news outlet, it seems to me that the overriding percentage of articles that deal with Israel and the "Palestinians" are radically in favor of the "Palestinians," not Israel.

In fact, if we look closely, we realize that at least in some cases, there are individual Jewish people who own and/or operate many of these media outlets. If so, why in almost all cases are they totally opposed to Israel itself? Why are these people *not* opposed to the "Palestinians"? There have been too many cases of managing editors (Jewish) who have come unglued because of others' support for Israel. Many secular Jews do not want Israel to have what she has, and they believe she should give up what she has so that the world can finally come to a peaceful solution to the Middle East problem.

In fact, many Jews fully believe that if Israel would simply give the "Palestinians" what they want, then peace would be at hand. Why do they believe this? Because these (secular) Jews do not want to see another Jewish holocaust take place. They do not want to see a repeat of WWII under Hitler's anti-Semitic regime.

Jews like George Soros – who, incidentally, worked for Hitler during WWII pointing the finger at other Jews – control a good portion of the media. Jews like Soros have no love loss for the state of Israel. They do not care whether it exists or does not exist, although when push comes to shove, they would prefer that it did not exist in the Middle East.

Soros and other secular Jewish individuals want peace with the Arabs/Muslims/"Palestinians." They are willing to throw the nation of Israel under the bus because it doesn't matter to them. These are the types of Jews who have control of a large portion of the media. It is not the Netanyahus who control what the media does. It is the secular Jewish person, who has managed to position him/herself so that they can slant the news against Israel. They believe that if they do that enough, the world's eye will not look favorably on the nation of Israel and Israel will then be forced to give up what they have now.

This is obviously a huge risk, because people like George Soros are still Jewish. They could receive some of the backlash; however, in Soros' case, his own history is clear: he thinks of himself first and is absolutely not above turning on his own countrymen for personal gain. The world does not think of Soros as Jewish. They simply see him as a multi-billionaire who allegedly controls the Obama Administration.

Since it is clear that Mr. Obama is set against Israel, then we can also surmise that Soros is as well. There is no way that Mr. Obama would go against Soros, and because of that it is certainly safe to assume that Mr. Obama is in line with Soros' thinking and his objectives.

So this idea that "the Jews" control the media and implicitly try to turn the world's sympathies toward or in favor of Israel is absolutely absurd. Unfortunately, people will continue to believe it simply because throughout Ezekiel alone, we learn that Israel will be a sore spot to many nations until the end.

The reactionary viewpoint of many who on one hand believe "the Jews" control the media, while at the same time believing that Israel is fully in the wrong and the other nations are simply defending themselves, is fully at odds with logic. That doesn't matter to most, though, because too many people have read and believe The Protocols of the Elders of Zion, a work that essentially states that the elite (read: "*the Jews*") have this plan to take over the world and have their fingers in everything.

It doesn't pan out. I fully believe that there is an "elite" that is trying to control things, but I also believe that the people who make up that "elite" consist of secular Jews AND Gentiles. George Soros is one of them, in my opinion, and we know that he is without doubt not in favor of the nation of Israel.

The people who make up the elite simply want to collectively rule the world, and the Bible is clear that they will get their chance to do that. In fact, out of this group another will arise who will be the "8th of out of the 7" and the "11th out of the ten." This is clear in Daniel, and while that used to confuse me years ago, I understand what it means now. The Antichrist will pop up out of the group and will begin his grab for world dominance.

Ezekiel 1 - 35

The Bible has a good deal to say about Israel, past, present, and future. For instance, the first 35 chapters deal with aspects of Israel's history that have already occurred, for the most part. We know this because we can simply compare these first 35 chapters with human history and see the events as they unfolded.

But let's talk about Ezekiel 36 – 39 for a few moments, because too many people who want to cast off Israel today seem to have no clue about this section (as well as numerous other sections) of God's Word as it relates to Israel.

Ezekiel 36

Though the first part of Ezekiel deals with events past, when we arrive at chapter 36, things change. We begin to look to the future. If for no other reason, we know this because here in chapter 36 God through the prophet Ezekiel begins to speak of a complete regeneration that will occur with the nation of Israel.

Most agree that this is yet future. Unfortunately, there are those who allegorize Scripture at this point (because it is future) and immediately change from dealing with Israel to the Church. So, up until and through chapter 35, the Bible is referring to Israel (actual Jews in this nation). But because of their penchant to allegorize or spiritualize Scripture, from 36 onward, all of a sudden "Israel" becomes the Church, even though it is the same language, God is still speaking to Ezekiel the prophet, and He (God) is still talking about Ezekiel's "people," who are Jewish. This does not matter to those who spiritualize the text, though, because it makes perfect sense to them. Does it? Not really, but that doesn't stop them.

Chapter 36 of Ezekiel begins by talking about the Mountains of Israel. Here, God is not even talking about people. He is talking about a physical place; a landmark, if you will. The Mountains of Israel pretty much run vertically through just about the entire land of Israel, right through the center.

The Mountains of Israel have been the centerpiece of many events that have occurred in actual Israel's true history. The opening verses of chapter 36 tell us that God says to Ezekiel that he should prophesy to these mountains. This is not allegorical. This is literal. Ezekiel is to prophesy to these mountains.

Notice, God does this because the enemy has spoken against these mountains (v. 2). It is because the enemy has spoken against these mountains that God steps in. God continues by stating, *"Because they made you desolate and swallowed you up on every side, so that you became the possession of the rest of the nations, and you are taken up by the lips of talkers and slandered by the people"* (vv. 2-3).

God is speaking TO the Mountains of Israel here. Currently, the Arabs believe that they are entitled to this same land. God says, nope, not on His watch. Yet these nations persevere.

God then states clearly what He plans on doing, and He specifically says that He is referring to the Mountains of Israel, the ravines and the valleys, and the areas that have become waste to the cities that many have forgotten about. God is not talking about ONE Jewish person here. He is referring only to the LAND that He gave the nation of Israel centuries ago.

Starting in verse five, God proclaims that because of His jealousy, He has spoken against all the other nations because of the way they treated – what, the Jews? No, it is because of the way these nations have trampled HIS Land. *"Therefore prophesy concerning the land of Israel and say to the mountains and to the hills, to the ravines and to the valleys, 'Thus says the Lord GOD, "Behold, I have spoken in My jealousy and in My wrath because you have endured the insults of the nations." Therefore thus says the Lord GOD, "I have sworn that surely the nations which are around you will themselves endure their insults. But you, O mountains of Israel, you will put forth your branches and bear your fruit for My people Israel; for they will soon come. For, behold, I am for you, and I will turn to you, and you will be cultivated and sown. I will multiply men on you, all the house of Israel, all of it; and the cities will be inhabited and the waste places will be rebuilt. I will multiply on you man and beast; and they will increase and be fruitful; and I will cause you to be inhabited as you were formerly and will treat you better than at the first. Thus you will know that I am the LORD."'"* (vv. 6-11).

Once again, God is speaking about the physical land areas of the nation of Israel. He has grown tired of the many nations running amok, doing whatever they think they can do to HIS Land.

It is not until verse 11 that God begins to speak of actual people. But God confirms the fact that He has heard the taunts and insults of all the nations (and that currently includes the United States under the Obama Administration). Because of this, God promises that the Land will have people in it and the nation that belongs there – Israel – will no longer stumble (cf. v. 15).

Then, beginning in verse 16, God confirms to Ezekiel that the NATION of Israel defiled His Land when they lived there. Because of that, God poured out His wrath (v. 18) on "them" (the nation) and He scattered them among the nations because they became idolaters just like their neighbors. It was God who scattered His people (v. 19). He judged them.

Notice also that these same people – after God scattered them among the nations – continued to profane His Name. Notice – and this is EXTREMELY important – that in verses 21-22, God says *"**But I had concern for My holy name,** which the house of Israel had profaned among the nations where they went. "Therefore say to the house of Israel, 'Thus says the Lord GOD, **"It is not for your sake, O house of Israel, that I am about to act, but for My holy name,** which you have profaned among the nations where you went."* (emphasis added)

Someone read one of my blogs at *studygrowknowblog.com* and wrote me saying that he was confident that today's Israel is not the promised people. I pointed out to him that his opinion has nothing to do with the truth of Scripture. The reality is that God seems to be fulfilling the latter end of Ezekiel, and because of that, He is concerned most with His Name. The people of Israel are secondary.

What people fail to realize is that Israel is the only nation God ever created. The rest of them simply happened based on Genesis 11 and elsewhere. Israel was specifically created by God as part of His plan of redemption. Though He has judged the nation and killed many people within it throughout Israel's history, one thing He has never done is destroyed the nation itself.

The secular nation of Israel is made up of Jews. Just as Paul explains in Romans 9-11, simply being Jewish does not guarantee salvation, or that the specific Jew is part of the true nation of Israel. This is the same with the Church. Just because someone attends a physical church does not necessarily mean they are part of the spiritual Church. God has always kept for Himself a Remnant of believers within the nation of Israel.

Today, that Remnant is hidden within the true Church. Once the Church is gone (through the Rapture), God will then turn His attention back to the people of Israel and begin refining them, and as He did many times in the Old Testament, He will purge the rebels from the nation. What He will be left with is a nation that is completely loyal to Him, because their eyes will be open and they will have realized their need for salvation that can only be found in Jesus.

Today, the nation of Israel is a nation, a group. God continues to protect Israel for no other reason than for the sake of His holy Name. He protects that Land over there for the same reason – for the sake of His holy Name.

Chapter 36 of Ezekiel continues to tell us that God began re-gathering His people back to that Land, and He emphasizes the fact that He does this solely for the sake of His Name. When He is through with Israel, He will have His loyal remnant and then *"'...I will vindicate the holiness of My great name which has been profaned among the nations, which you have profaned in their midst. Then the nations will know that I am the LORD,' declares the Lord GOD, 'when I prove Myself holy among you in their sight'"* (cf. v. 23).

People mistakenly believe that God does everything He does in the Middle East because of the Jewish people. Nope. He does what He does for the sake of His holy Name. He will USE the nation of Israel to return glory to His Name. He will use the nation of Israel to show the world that the promises He made thousands of years ago to Abraham will be fulfilled, and they will NOT be fulfilled in the Church, but through Israel.

The ONLY way God can restore absolute glory to His Name is by using Israel (both the land *and* the people) to do it. Why? It is because the nation of Israel brought dishonor and disgrace to His Name in the first place. People who say that Ezekiel 36 onward is referring to the Church have no clue.

It is clear from Chapter 36 alone that God will restore His Name. The Church did not slander God's Name. It was ISRAEL that slandered His Name. The world will pay attention when Israel is restored to the Land and they ultimately turn in true worship to the very God they rejected 2,000 years ago.

You see, what is fascinating about Israel is that it changes with each generation. To God, though, He sees a *nation*, not individual people. God still holds Israel responsible for slandering His Name. He still holds that nation responsible for rejecting the Messiah. Yet, the Jewish people alive today were not alive during the Old Testament times, nor were they the ones who actually rejected Jesus and nailed Him to the cross. It was the nation of Israel through the leaders of Israel who did these things, and it is the nation of Israel that has been judged because of these things.

But God – having judged the nation of Israel in the past – will restore this same nation (though the people in it change, it is STILL the same nation) – to its former glory. Why will God do this? Because He is planning on restoring the glory and honor to His Name that the NATION (through their leaders) of Israel destroyed.

It is all very simple, except to those who are unable to see it. These people either do not study Scripture or they tend to allegorize it. If not that, then they spend too much time reading secular news from the liberal media. What does the secular news have to say about God's Word? Nothing good.

Folks, God WILL restore Israel's glory, and He will do it for one reason and one reason only: for the sake of His holy Name. That is the reason. There is NO other reason at all. It is not because He loves Israel and hates the rest of the world. It is not because He loves Jews and hates Arabs. This is not true. It is because He will restore the lost glory and honor to His holy Name and He has been doing it on the back of the nation of Israel.

We will deal with this more as we go through the remainder of Ezekiel 36 and then get into 37, 38, and 39. It is extremely important that people stop looking at things through human eyes and begin to understand what God is doing and why He is doing it.

This nation is on a crash course with God. We are moving in the absolute wrong direction. At every turn, Mr. Obama is throwing Israel under the bus. In his last speech, he clearly said that Israel should return to *pre*-1967 borders. Then, he lied about that and said, "What I meant was that both the Palestinians and the Jews should decide their own borders" (my paraphrase). If he had meant that, he could have easily said that, but he did not say that.

God will not sit idly by and watch human beings divvy up *His Land*. It simply will not happen. According to Ezekiel 36, God put Israel out of the land, but then began bringing them back. *"For I will take you from the nations, gather you from all the lands and bring you into your own land. Then I will sprinkle clean water on you, and you will be clean; I will cleanse you from all your filthiness and from all your idols. Moreover, I will give you a new heart and put a new spirit within you; and I will remove the heart of stone from your flesh and give you a heart of flesh. I will put My Spirit within you and cause you to walk in My statutes, and you will be careful to observe My ordinances.* **You will live in the land that I gave to your forefathers**; *so you will be My people, and I will be your God"* (cf. vv. 24-28; emphasis added).

It seems clear enough that God is the one who brought the Jews back to the Land in 1948, yet people argue about this or that and say the U.N. shouldn't have done this, or it was Britain that did it, etc. According to Scripture, GOD did it, and certainly He used nations and the situation, but ultimately, He takes credit for it. The people who firmly believe that Israel (the nation) has no right to the Land better be extremely careful. If Scripture is correct (which it is), then those who stand in opposition to Israel right now are in effect opposing God as well, and that is not a good place to be.

Verses 24 – 28 describe a process that unfolds for us in the latter portion of Ezekiel 36 and especially chapter 37. It is a process, not an instantaneous happening or event.

The first part of this began in 1948 when God began re-gathering Jewish people back to the Land. Why did He do that? Because it was the first step in Him ultimately returning glory and honor to His holy Name.

You people who are opposed to Israel had better humble yourselves and repent, because you are sinning by standing opposed to God and His will. If you are unable to see that, it is because you have never asked Him to open your eyes to the truth. Please do so now.

2

Resurrection of Israel

We have discussed the fact that when God initially kicked the nation of Israel out of the Land of Israel, He did so for a *purpose*. That purpose had everything to do with His judgment against a people that exploited His holy Name and brought absolute dishonor to it. They became idolaters and suffered His wrath because of that practice. The final insult was when the leaders of the nation of Israel rejected the Messiah. Within forty years of that event, in which the crucifixion of Jesus took place, Jerusalem and the Temple were destroyed due to the attack of Roman armies.

Surviving Jewish people scattered, leaving the Land of Israel far behind.

In spite of what many people believe, God's plan for Israel did not end there, though. His plan reached way into the future, to the point in time when He would return them to that same Land from which He had removed them as He began to gather them from the nations around the world. This began His final fulfillment of what He promised to do with the Land and the nation of Israel in the final days of human history.

God's promises to nation and the Land of Israel are clearly seen in the first 28 verses of Ezekiel 36. He continues in verses 29-30 by saying, *"Moreover, I will save you from all your uncleanness; and I will call for the grain and multiply it, and I will not bring a famine on you. I will multiply the fruit of the tree and the produce of the field, so that you will not receive again the disgrace of famine among the nations."*

The point of this is that God will thoroughly bless Israel, once again allowing the Land to flow with milk and honey after He has restored the nation of Israel to the Land. Once again, He clearly and succinctly notes His reason for doing this: *"Then you will remember your evil ways and your deeds that were not good, and you will loathe yourselves in your own sight for your iniquities and your abominations"* (v. 31). The reason God decided to restore the Land *and* the nation within it has nothing to do with the people of Israel. God wants the people of Israel to know what they have done. He wants them to understand without doubt the tremendous dishonor the people of Israel have brought to His holy Name. He wants them to literally become undone because of it. He wants them to realize the result of their actions.

This is all for a *purpose*. It is not so that God can sit back and enjoy their sorrow. God simply wants them to understand that in spite of their mistreatment and misrepresentation of Him, His promises stand for all eternity. Those promises *will* find fulfillment.

"'Thus says the Lord GOD, "On the day that I cleanse you from all your iniquities, I will cause the cities to be inhabited, and the waste places will be rebuilt. The desolate land will be cultivated instead of being a desolation in the sight of everyone who passes by. They will say, 'This desolate land has become like the garden of Eden; and the waste, desolate and ruined cities are fortified and inhabited.' Then the nations that are left round about you will know that I, the LORD, have rebuilt the ruined places and planted that which was desolate; I, the LORD, have spoken and will do it.""" (Ezekiel 36:33-36).

God repeats Himself here as He seems to do often in Scripture because He is emphasizing a point. If we follow through on the logical flow of God's plan, it looks like this:

1. God will cleanse the nation from their sin
2. He will create a situation that allows them to live in the cities of Israel
3. Because they come back to Israel, the old cities will be rebuilt
4. The Land that laid bare and desolate for centuries will bring forth new life
5. People who see this will marvel at the transformation that has come over the Land
6. It is because of this process (outlined in steps a through e) that honor will be restored to God's holy Name
7. People will know that in spite of all the odds against them, Jewish people not only came back to the Land, but rebuilt cities and planted new gardens as a result of God
8. The glory will go to God, not Israel or any other nation

We see this process happening now within the Land of Israel. Since *before* 1948 Jewish people began moving back into the Land they once possessed. During 1948, Israel once again became a nation.

That which was dead came *alive*. No one thought it would happen. All bets would have been against Israel ever becoming a nation again. Yet it *did* happen, in spite of all the odds. From that time, regardless of all the wars, the skirmishes, the rockets, the terrorism against Israel, and every country (except Canada at this writing) turning against Israel, that tiny nation came into existence and has continued to exist.

Not only has Israel continued to exist, but the *Land* of Israel has begun again to flourish, due directly to the return of Jewish people to their homeland and the beginning of the *fulfillment* of Ezekiel chapter 36. The Land once again has begun flowing with milk and honey. Towns have been rebuilt. Gardens have been planted. The Land of Israel looks totally different today than it did when the Jewish people began returning to it decades ago.

This process has taken well over 60 years and is not yet complete. Jewish people continue to return to their homeland because God is calling them to that Land that He purposefully kept from them for centuries.

When His plan is complete, the world will glorify God because of it. The idea that Ezekiel 36 onward is somehow connected to the Church that the Holy Spirit gave birth to in Acts 2 and not Israel, is absurd. The language of Ezekiel is very specific and the only way to say that chapters 36 - 39 relate to the Church is to *allegorize* the text. There is nothing in the text that should prompt anyone to do that, because we have been seeing the fulfillment of Ezekiel 36 take place before our eyes in this generation.

God's plan of redemption includes redemption for the *Land* of Israel as well as the *nation* of Israel. The redemption for the Jewish people as a nation will come to them the same way it comes to all of us, and that is through the life, death, and resurrection of Jesus. Jewish people who become saved today become part of the authentic

Church. Once the Church is taken in the Rapture, the only people left in the world will be *unsaved*, whether they are Jewish or Gentile. No one who is an authentic Christian will be "left behind" after the Rapture has occurred.

Life does not stop after the Rapture. What begins then is the final phase of God's plan of salvation for those in the world who *will* become authentic Christians, and this includes His redemptive plan for the nation of Israel. As a unit, all those who have been chosen as the Remnant of Israel (before the foundations of the world) will come to a point of realization in which they will understand whom their leaders rejected over 2,000 years ago. They will see the truth about Jesus *collectively*, as a nation (and again, I am referring to the Remnant here).

It is the same with those Gentiles who were not taken in the Rapture. They will remain, and according to the book of Revelation, multitudes will be saved, many losing their life for Jesus with the tremendous wave of persecution that is perpetrated against humanity under the dictatorship of the Antichrist. This is the Tribulation period.

So God's plan to redeem all who will call on His Name will continue even after the Rapture occurs. I've heard people say, *"Oh, but come on, you're saying that God will give these people a second chance!"* Of course I am. The first time I heard about Jesus, I did not become a Christian. It wasn't until I was thirteen years old that I committed my life to Christ because I had finally reached a point of realizing my need for salvation. I have no idea how many times I heard the gospel presented to me during those thirteen years before the truth finally dawned on me.

Verses 37 – 38 of Ezekiel 36 tell us that God will increase the number of men in Israel like a flock or a herd. These people will know that He is God. This is solely because God will open their eyes to that truth, which is the only way anyone can know that He is God. Whether a person is Jewish or Gentile, salvation comes the exact same way to every person. The timing may be different, but knowledge of the truth comes from God.

Ezekiel 37
The 37th chapter of Ezekiel is a chapter that most who have read or studied Scripture have at least heard of, and it is referred to as the Valley of Dry Bones because God shows Ezekiel the prophet a valley that is filled with bones. These bones are so dead and have been dead for so long that they are literally dry.

Have you ever been walking in a field or in the desert and you come across a skull or bone of an animal? It can quickly be apparent that the skull or bone has been there for some time if the bone or skull is completely devoid of skin or hair or anything. If there is nothing left but bone and it has been bleached by the sun, that indicates age. All of this information tells us that the particular bone has been there for quite some time.

Like any living thing, an animal that dies goes through a process of decay. The decay slowly rots the carcass of that animal. Other animals may come and eat part of the animal. After many days, the bones will have been stripped of anything edible. Months later, the bone or skull will begin to change color from a natural bone color to a whitish shade. The longer it lies in the sun, the whiter it becomes. Eventually, it begins to turn to dust and slowly breaks apart as it continues to lie in the sun.

In this chapter, God shows Ezekiel a valley of bones that have clearly been there for some time. *"The hand of the LORD was upon me, and He brought me out by the Spirit of the LORD and set me down in the middle of the valley; and it was full of bones. He caused me to pass among them round about, and behold, there were very many on the surface of the valley; and lo, they were* **very dry**. *He said to me, 'Son of* man, can these bones live?' And I answered, 'O Lord GOD, You know.' Again He said to me, 'Prophesy over these bones and say to them, "O dry bones, hear the word of the LORD. Thus says the Lord GOD to these bones, 'Behold, I will cause breath to enter you that you may come to life. I will put sinews on you, **make flesh grow back on you**, cover you with skin and put breath in you that you may come alive; and you will know that I am the LORD.'"*

"So I prophesied as I was commanded; and as I prophesied, there was a noise, and behold, a rattling; and the bones came together, bone to its bone. And I looked, and behold, sinews were on them, and flesh grew and skin covered them; but there was no breath in them" (Ezekiel 37:1-8; emphasis added).

Notice that Ezekiel points out that the bones were *"very dry."* This tells us that they had gone through the process of decay and were simply waiting for the last thing to happen – the breaking down of those bones into dust.

Obviously, Ezekiel is seeing bones that were alive at one point and are now quite dead, but not fully decayed. God asks Ezekiel an important question about the bones. Can the bones live?

Ezekiel responds that God knows. God then tells Ezekiel to prophesy to the bones and God tells Ezekiel what to say to them. Ezekiel obeys and he tells the bones that they are to hear the Word of the Lord. Ultimately, God says through the prophet that He will put breath back into them and they shall live.

God will put sinews on the bones to connect them one to the other, and then flesh to cover the bones. Notice that God is going to do this to bring the bones to life, and also understand that God says that when He is through, the bones will *know* that He is God.

God speaks about the breath *first*, but that is the last thing that happens to the bones. It's the last thing that happened to Adam as well. God created the man by forming his body out of dust and *then* He breathed into Adam the breath of life and Adam became a living spirit, as we read in Genesis 2, verse 7.

Just as God created Adam from the dust of the earth and breathed life into his body, so will God give life to that which was, by all accounts, fully dead. God here is referring to the *Land* and the *nation of Israel*. He is not referring to the Church at all, because the Church was never *dead*, then resurrected. The church was not born until the second chapter of Acts on the day of Pentecost.

It is clear from history that the nation of Israel literally *died* off the map. However, God was not content to leave that nation dead, and here in Chapter 37, He promises to bring Israel *back* from the dead. This He began doing just after World War I with the Zionist movement. Following World War II, it was clear to Jewish people that they must have their own nation again. Though they believed this was simply a pragmatic course of action to preserve themselves, it is clear from Scripture that God is the One who made this happen.

So the first step in the process of reviving Israel is complete. From that point, God tells Ezekiel about the next phase. *"Then He said to me, 'Prophesy to the breath, prophesy, son of man, and say to the breath, "Thus says the Lord GOD, 'Come from the four winds, O breath, and breathe on these slain, that they come to life".' So I prophesied as He commanded me, and the breath came into them, and they came to life and stood on their feet, an exceedingly great army"* (Ezekiel 37:9-10).

So after the bones were covered first with sinews and muscles, they were clothed in skin. But that alone does not make a living being. Only the breath of life will cause that being to actually live. God uses the wind from the four corners of the earth (*"four winds"*) to breathe into this great army of non-living bodies.

Once the breath comes into these bodies, they come *alive* and prove it by standing on their feet. The entire implication of Ezekiel 36 and 37 so far is that *what was once dead is now alive again.* The bones that were dried out obviously represent something that was once *alive* – living and breathing. They died, leaving only decaying, dried out bones as a remembrance of what once lived. With those bones, God chose to build them back up and cause breath to return to them.

Since it is clear that the bones were once living and are made alive again, this could not at all be referring to the Church since the Church had never been born *and then died* only to rise again. I realize that many today see the fulfillment of this in the Church. They make a connection between those dead bones and the fact that they became alive again and they say that once they became alive again, that is representative of the Church as the final phase of God's plan of redemption.

The problem, though, is that verse eleven is very clear. *"Then He said to me, 'Son of man, these bones are **the whole house of Israel**; behold, they say, "Our bones are dried up and our hope has perished. We are completely cut off"'"* (emphasis added). The only way to get around the obvious meaning here is to take the phrase *"the whole house of Israel"* and apply it to the Church. This can only be done through allegorizing the text, as previously mentioned. To take the text literally means that God is speaking of the actual nation of Israel.

There is a difference between taking something literally and taking something literal*istically*. In the former, we understand that God is using a type of parable or metaphor to present His meaning. We understand that though God is referring to a valley of dead bones, He is simply using that picture as a vehicle through which He explains to Ezekiel (and to us) that the bones simply *represent* the House of Israel. The bones are *not* the actual house of Israel. He is showing – through the prophet – how He will *revive* Israel, a nation that died some time ago. Ezekiel is seeing a vision, and from that vision, a lesson from God. God uses the parable or story to define what He is *literally* going to do with the *Land* as well as the *nation* of Israel.

If we were to take the parable literal*istically*, we would have to say that bones *are* the house of Israel. That is absurd and makes no sense within the context. Taking the words literally allows us to understand *God's* meaning within the parable He is speaking to the prophet. The interesting thing about metaphors and parables is that they generally have one meaning.

Verse eleven clearly has God stating, "*...these bones are the whole house of Israel.*" This puts to rest the idea that somehow, if we allegorize the text, we can make it mean that God is really saying, "*...these bones represent something I will do in the future through my Son, and it will be called the Church.*" Again, this is a silly and unnecessary abstraction of God's Word that has no basis in fact.

It is very clear – or *should* be – that what has transpired in the Middle East is due directly to the work that God has been and continues to do among the people of Israel and in the Land of Israel. This does not mean there are two forms of salvation, one for Jewish people and one for everyone else. This concept is rejected based on the text where Jesus says He will not return until they cry out for Him to do so (cf. Matthew 23:39): "*For I say to you, from now on you will not see Me until you say, 'BLESSED IS HE WHO COMES IN THE NAME OF THE LORD'!*" It is obvious from this text and the context that Jesus is speaking to Jewish people here. The Remnant of Israel *will* one day realize their sin and the terrible mistake their religious leaders made in rejecting Jesus. It will be on that day that they will turn to the One they rejected, begging for His help. In essence, then, they will turn to Jesus, realizing that He was who He said He was, and will receive the salvation that comes only from Him.

So in Ezekiel 36 and 37, God has been outlining His plan to restore and redeem the nation of Israel as well as the Land itself. He means what He says, and it should not be difficult at all to see that from 1948 onward until today and beyond, God has been doing exactly what He originally said He would do through the prophet Ezekiel.

In verses 12 through 14 God tells the prophet to *"...Therefore prophesy and say to them, 'Thus says the Lord GOD, "Behold, I will open your graves and cause you to come up out of your graves, My people; and I will bring you into the land of Israel. Then you will know that I am the LORD, when I have opened your graves and caused you to come up out of your graves, My people. I will put My Spirit within you and you will come to life, and I will place you on your own land. Then you will know that I, the LORD, have spoken and done it," declares the LORD'."*

God is speaking about actual *people* at this point because in this vision that Ezekiel sees, the bones have become actual, living beings. God is saying that He will resurrect them by opening their "graves" and causing them to come up from those "graves." He then says He will put His Spirit within them and He will place them in the very Land He promised to them through Abraham.

This is the process that God has undertaken, and over the past five to six decades since Israel became a nation, God has been and continues to bring His people back to the Land. Once He has completed that process, He will *then* be able to put His Spirit within them. But is God talking about the *entire* race of Jews? Even though millions of Jewish people have gone back to the Land of Israel, God has His *Remnant* and only those who make up that Remnant will be given His Spirit.

Once the Millennial reign of Jesus begins, it is this group of Jewish people as God's Remnant that will go in and fully possess the Land that God originally gave to them through Abraham. Unless you understand these portions of God's Word allegorically, it is impossible to mistake God's meaning: He will complete His plan for the Land and nation of Israel for the sake of His holy Name, whether anyone likes it or not.

3

Beyond the Valley of Bones

The process that God has used to begin to bring Israel back to life has been a long one, as far as humanity is concerned. With God, not so much, since He is neither governed by time, or exists within it.

Today's Israel has been a long time in the making. Since the destruction of Jerusalem and the Temple in A.D. 70, it took centuries for the situation to develop that would not only allow Israel to once again come back to life, but encourage Jewish people to begin resettling the Land they once possessed.

Of course, the world is not interested in this because they are more interested in simply having "peace" in the Middle East. They live under the false delusion that if peace was gained in that area of the world, then this whole world would live under the banner of peaceful co-existence. This is a pipedream at best. It will not happen until Jesus actually rules the world.

Does this mean we should not try? Of course not, but it *does* mean that we should not presume to believe that God's Word is not valid because we think we have a better way of doing things.

In the last chapter, we dealt with the fact that God exhorted Ezekiel the prophet to prophesy over a valley filled with dead, dry bones. These bones had once been alive and God was preparing to bring them back to life. He had a process, and that process is now coming to pass.

That should cause people to stop and wonder about God and His Word. If this – Ezekiel 36-37 – is exactly what is happening in this world, then we are privileged to live in a generation that is seeing God's Word come alive. What an absolutely astounding privilege it is, too!

It means that God's Word is true. It means that He is not finished with Israel. It means that all the rest of the prophecies in His Word that have yet to find fulfillment *will* be fulfilled. Unfortunately, along with this comes the strong delusion that God says He will send on those who continue to reject His Word (cf. 2 Thessalonians 2:11). Because they are not interested in the truth, God will keep them from it so that they will not even find it accidentally.

What we read in the previous verses of both chapters 36 and 37 of Ezekiel tells us that God is fully in charge. He will put life back into a dead nation. He will restore their fortunes. He will exchange their hard-heartedness for a heart that is open to Him and turned toward

Him. God will literally place His Spirit within that Remnant of Jewish people who will yearn to know Him and His truth. This is exactly what He does with everyone who comes to Him seeking His truth and salvation. These Jewish people are no different.

To view this section of Ezekiel as referring to the Church does tremendous damage to the text. The Church exists today. Do you see that God is proving that He is holy to the world *through* the Church? I don't. This is not to say that the Church is not holy, because it *is* holy according to Paul in various places throughout the New Testament.

People wrongly believe that the Church needs to be purified today. No, the Church *is pure* and it is based solely on the work of Jesus on the cross. Just as His blood saves me from eternal death by washing me clean, His blood also cleanses each person who trusts in Him.

Authentic Christians know that we are clean. We also know that our sins have been completely *cancelled*, past, present, and future. He promises that He will not remember our sin (Isaiah 43:25). Paul tells us that we are already seated with Christ in the heavenlies (cf. Ephesians 2). These truths are difficult for us to appreciate, yet they are fact.

Authentic Christians are forgiven, cleansed from all sin, justified, and purified. The Church is made up of authentic Christians. It is not made up of people who simply go to church, pray, sing hymns, or even study their Bibles. The true Church consists only of people who have been washed in the blood of Jesus. Those who merely *profess* to be Christians, but are not, have no part in Jesus. They are not His, He does not know them, and they are not part of the true Church.

This is part of the problem today. People constantly mistake the true Church with the visible church. The visible church consists of people who are authentic believers as well as those who are professing believers, but have never had that true conversion. They have never been born again, or born from above (John 3). They may fully believe themselves to be authentic Christians, but without that new birth, they are not.

The world looks at the visible church today and scoffs. They laugh because of the obvious hypocrisy that is rampant without the visible church. However, this hypocrisy does not extend to the true Church that the Holy Spirit birthed on the day of Pentecost.

It is because of the visible church that the world cannot see God. They laugh and carry on because the visible church has little power to change anyone's viewpoint. It is the true Church that has the power to change, because the Holy Spirit is building all authentic believers into a body that is fit for Jesus.

The folks that argue that the Church is the subject of Ezekiel 37 are wrong, in my opinion. They believe that it is the Church that will bring glory to God by forcing all the nations to recognize Him as God. This is not happening, folks, and it is not happening because of the visible church, which is the only thing the world can see. Because of it, they are not impressed.

However, if God were to take a nation that He created and judged on many occasions and bring that dead nation back to life, the world would absolutely take notice. The more God involves Himself in protecting the Land of Israel along with the people of Israel, the more the world will notice.

Today, all eyes are on the Middle East and have been for decades. The world waits with baited breath to learn what is going to happen next in that section of the world. They tune to that frequency and wonder.

As God's plan for the Land and the nation of Israel continues to unfold, the world will be forced to notice. Against all odds, the nation of Israel, though initially overcome by enemy forces in 1967, gained the upper hand and took more land than she had prior to the start of the Six-Day War. Israel's enemies were so convinced of their victory that they did not consider the fact that God was with Israel.

Was God with Israel because Jewish people are more loved than non-Jewish? Not according to what we have learned so far in Ezekiel.

Why then did Israel gain the victory over her enemies? It is simply due to the fact that God is using Israel to gain the glory for Himself. Since the world is so convinced that Israel has no right to exist in the Middle East, the fact that they won a decisive battle during the Six-Day War made many aware of something else that was going on there.

Tiny Israel was able to defend herself against enemies more powerful than herself *and* gained more Land because of it. How could that happen unless God was trying to prove something *through* Israel? Isn't that what He said?

4

The Northern Invasion

This next part of the book of Ezekiel, chapters 38 - 39 is interesting for a number of reasons. Some theologians place this event at the end of the Tribulation period, referring to it as Armageddon. Others teach that the scenario described in chapters 38 and 39 take place *prior* to the start of the Tribulation period. While it is difficult to be dogmatic about it, there are certain indicators that can help us make a decision. One thing is clear: a group of nations gather together for the sole purpose of attacking Israel, with dire results…to *themselves*.

This chapter is one of those chapters that highlight the fact that God – without doubt – is in full control of all things. Many people prefer not to think of things this way. They do not see God in charge of much if anything, and the reason for that has to do with their faulty understanding of the exact nature of free will. Many believe that because people have free will, they therefore choose what they can and cannot do, or what they will or will not do. While this is true, this has no impact at all on God, as if He somehow needs to wait until *we* make a decision before He can act. This is absurd.

Beings with free will always resort to rebelling against authority. We will always use our free will to turn against God because having to submit to someone else grates on us. In order for God to accomplish what He chooses to accomplish, it is merely a matter of Him locating the person who is already prone to do what He (God) wants accomplished. In that way, God is not going *against* that person's free will (such as it is) and simply winds up using that person's predilection to carry out His purposes.

Judas was chosen by God for the task that he (Judas) eventually contrived and carried out: the betrayal of Jesus. Had God intervened and overrode Judas' own will and desires there might be some reason to say that God was unfair. In essence, though, a couple of things keep God from actually being unfair (as far as our severely limited human perspective is concerned). First of all, all human beings are *sinful,* and because of that we wind up doing things we really do not want to do. We do them because of our own inner propensities, temptation, or both. This also colors our view of things.

Satan tries to prompt us to use our free will to rebel against God consistently. He is often victorious. Our sin nature has automatically placed us at odds with God, so Satan merely uses that, along with outward stimuli, to get us to do *his* (Satan's) will. In truth, one wonders to what extent we actually have free will in the end.

We have sinned, therefore we are sinners. This is what we do, and even those of us who have become authentically saved will sin from time to time. Hopefully, the longer we have been authentic Christians, the less we will sin; but we will never be free of the desire to sin until we physically leave this life, trading in our sin nature for a glorified, Christ-like nature.

Because we are sinners, the natural tendency is to do the things that do not please God. Whether we listen to and give into our own evil desires or whether we listen to and give into Satan's, the result is the same. It is the carrying out of sinful practices.

For God to carry out the first part of Ezekiel 38, all He has to do is put a person in a position of authority and leadership who for one reason or another hates the idea that Israel exists. Because this person hates Israel, the tendency may be to constantly think of ways to overcome that nation, taking the spoils that Israel has and bringing them to their own nation or country. Let's take a look at the first six verses of Ezekiel 38 to see what's happening.

"And the word of the LORD came to me saying, 'Son of man, set your face toward Gog of the land of Magog, the prince of Rosh, Meshech and Tubal, and prophesy against him and say, "Thus says the Lord GOD, 'Behold, I am against you, O Gog, prince of Rosh, Meshech and Tubal. I will turn you about and put hooks into your jaws, and I will bring you out, and all your army, horses and horsemen, all of them splendidly attired, a great company with buckler and shield, all of them wielding swords; Persia, Ethiopia and Put with them, all of them with shield and helmet; Gomer with all its troops; Beth-togarmah from the remote parts of the north with all its troops—many peoples with you"'" (Ezekiel 38:1-6).

Notice that God is telling Ezekiel to prophesy *against* "him." The "him" in this text is referring to "Gog." We have learned that this term is merely a title, not the specific name of a person. It is like calling someone "Captain," "Admiral," or "General." It does not tell us who this "Gog" is, and some folks even disagree over the area of "Magog." Most have believed this to be Russia because as the text will tell us in verse 15, this Gog comes out of the far north against Israel.

Whether it's Russia or some other nation, the important thing is what God says about Gog. He says through Ezekiel to tell Gog that He (God) is against him. This Gog is the *"prince of Rosh, Meshech and Tubal."* He is a leader of an expansive area and because of that has many resources available to him, including a powerful army and a number of powerful allies.

But notice: because God is against Gog, something is going to happen, and in spite of the fact that Gog thinks he has come up with the idea, it is clear that God Himself is the one who sets things in motion. God says, *"I will turn you about and put hooks into your jaws, and I will bring you out, and all your army, horses and horsemen, all of them splendidly attired, a great company with buckler and shield, qll of them wielding swords..."*

Here, God is stating specifically that the actions of Gog, along with his army, will be the direct result of God's plan. At the same time, we learn a bit further on that Gog will think he had the idea because it is something he has wanted to do for some time (cf. v.10). We will get to this shortly.

It is not just Gog, the prince of Rosh (quite possibly a term meaning "chief" as in "chief prince of Meshech and Tubal), Meshech (possibly nation[s] from central or western Asia Minor), and Tubal (eastern Asia Minor) that attack Israel. Apparently, Persia (modern day Iran), Ethiopia, and Put (Libya), along with Beth-togarmah (probably the southeastern part of Turkey near the Syrian border, as noted by Ryrie), and Gomer (either Germany or parts of Asia Minor) will join Gog together in an attempted invasion of Israel.

The reality is that this represents a very large group of soldiers or armies from a variety of places in that part of the globe which, under the leadership of Gog, join together with one purpose. That purpose is to attack and defeat Israel. Since God is the One who takes credit for this insurgency, we can only assume that in this case at least, this attempted invasion will fail. He has something that He is going to prove not only to Gog, but to the other nations that join with him in this venture against Israel.

In verses 7 – 9 of Ezekiel 38, God describes for us through the prophet what this attempted invasion will look like. *"Be prepared, and prepare yourself, you and all your companies that are assembled about you, and be a guard for them. After many days you will be summoned; in the latter years you will come into the land that is restored from the sword, whose inhabitants have been gathered from many nations to the mountains of Israel which had been a continual waste; but its people were brought out from the nations, and they are living securely, all of them. You will go up, you will come like a storm; you will be like a cloud covering the land, you and all your troops, and many peoples with you."*

God is actually encouraging Gog to go through his preparation to make sure that he will believe he is fully equipped to handle any resistance that Israel may put up against him and his troops. Note that God says that Gog will be "summoned" and this will occur in "the latter years." The sense is that toward the end of human history, God will move Gog to gather his troops and forces and move against Israel. This event has yet to occur in history.

God then segues into a description of Israel at the time when Gog is "summoned" by God to attack Israel. God makes a number of statements about Israel's condition at the time of the attack:

1. Were restored from the sword
2. People were gathered from many nations to Israel

3. Previous to this, the Land was a constant waste; desolate
4. Again, God emphasizes that the people were brought from other nations
5. The people live securely

In essence, this describes Israel of today, 2011. There was great fighting for centuries until in 1948 Israel was given the chance to become a nation once again. At that point, they put down their swords (and swords here is merely a reference to weapons used in war. It does not necessarily mean actual swords) and began to plant and cultivate the Land. Up until that point, this same Land was desolate. There was nothing there. It was simply soil and desert.

With respect to the people of Israel living securely, what this means is that they believe they have the power, might, and technology to overcome whatever their enemies throw at them. It does not necessarily mean that they are living securely as if they do not fear ever being attacked.

In fact, even before Israel became a nation again in 1948, the people of Israel have known what it means to fight for their rights, their independence. Since becoming a nation, the turmoil has been constant. Whether they have been on the receiving end of constant artillery or rockets landing in their own backyards, or entering into a true war like the Six-Day War of 1967, the Israelites have known what it means to protect what is theirs. They are not stupid people, who unblinkingly believe that they have no enemies or that no one wants to hurt them or take their Land. They *live* with this constancy on a daily basis. Yet they are secure in the knowledge that they would be able to put up a good fight to keep enemies from taking what now belongs to Israel. That is the meaning of secure.

I live securely with my family in our home. By that, I don't mean I do not believe that no one would ever seek to break into my house and try to steal things from me. It is for that reason that I have locks on the windows and doors. When we leave for the day, all of those individual locks are used to make our home secure. If I really believed that no one would ever try to steal from me, I would never worry about closing the garage door. I would keep the doors and windows unlocked, whether I was home or not.

Living securely means that a person believes they are protected from outside forces who might wish to do harm. Whether it's a burglar or something else, we have made our home as burglar-proof as possible so that when we go to sleep at night or are away during the day, we consider the chance of someone breaking in remote. At the same time, we know that all of our actions have not guaranteed that we will never experience that unpleasantness.

A good many people go through their days thinking that evil will not touch them. It will always happen to someone else, not them. They will not be hurt or killed in an auto accident. They will not be mugged, beaten, raped, or murdered. That happens to other people. That is not living securely. It is living in a fantasy.

When I get in my car, the first thing I do is lock my doors. It is amazing to me how many people do not do this simple thing which creates a deterrent. When I'm walking someplace, I am constantly aware of my surroundings. When I am home, I may leave the front door open, but the security screen is closed and locked. This causes me to feel *secure* about my environment. It is *because* I know that things can happen that I take precautions.

This is Israel today. She is surrounded by Arab nations who hate her and want her gone. These nations do not believe there is room for the state of Israel in "their" own area of the world. They hate Israel and Islam teaches that Jews should be killed. That is considered an honorable thing to Allah. The truth of the matter is that in spite of these constant threats, Israel is fairly secure because of her armies, her Navy, and the technology through which Israel is protected. That is living securely.

It is in this type of situation in which Israel currently exists that Gog will consider attacking Israel. After all, this is what happened to start the Six-Day War in 1967. The nations that came against Israel did so on the Sabbath. They were overconfident. They believed that if they attacked Israel on the Sabbath, she would have no chance to defend herself.

This was the case initially, but over time, the tables were turned, allowing Israel to not only gain the upper hand, but gain more Land. That Land, for the most part, is still part of today's Israel, and the Arab nations surrounding Israel do not like it; yet they are the ones who attacked Israel in the first place.

When Gog decides to turn against Israel, his armies will be so large that the dirt cloud from his oncoming invasion will cover the Land, quite possibly darkening the entire visible sky. This is a large army, folks.

There is some argument about whether or not Gog will lead his troops on actual *horses*. This is what it states in verse 15. Do we have to *literally* understand these to be horses, or is this a general term that is used throughout Scripture (like "swords") to imply war? Though I believe God meant this part of Ezekiel to refer to these latter days, the first people to hear about this were the people of Ezekiel's day, the Israelites. Those people knew of horses, bows, arrows, shields, and bucklers as normal instruments used in warfare. They would not have known about tanks, heat-seeking missiles, helicopters, jets, and other modern day weaponry.

I think it is safe to say that though God used the term "horses" in describing Gog's army and how they would move against Israel, it is very likely that this is used to literally refer to the general sense of war-related vehicles and armaments. Today, it is highly doubtful that horses would be used in an attack such as one of this magnitude; unless, of course, that part of the world experienced a massive EMP (electro-magnetic pulse), knocking out everything that runs on some type of electricity.

Horses require food and water. Tanks, jets, and other modern weaponry require some form of fuel (as well as electricity), which is easy enough to obtain in the Middle East. God seems to simply be speaking in general terms here, terms that Ezekiel and his people would understand to refer to things used in times of war.

The point God is making here is not what type of vehicle Gog and his troops will use in their attempted invasion of Israel. The real point is the *size* of the total army. This is going to be a huge affair, one that will not be hidden. The army will be so large that the dust trail from the vehicles will darken the sky and be noticed for miles.

Certainly, in today's day and age of lightning fast technology, the attempted invasion will be picked up and carried by satellites, which will then transmit their signals/pictures/videos to TVs, phones, and computers. No mention of these things is noted in the text, but it can be implied that something on such a large scale as this would not go unnoticed by the world.

Verses 10-13 tell us the reason for this attempted invasion, realizing of course that God Himself sets things in motion. As far as Gog is concerned, he will not be aware that God has set things in motion. He will think he came up with the idea and will have a specific reason for doing what he will do.

"Thus says the Lord GOD, 'It will come about on that day, that thoughts will come into your mind and you will devise an evil plan, and you will say, "I will go up against the land of unwalled villages. I will go against those who are at rest, that live securely, all of them living without walls

and having no bars or gates, to capture spoil and to seize plunder, to turn your hand against the waste places which are now inhabited, and against the people who are gathered from the nations, who have acquired cattle and goods, who live at the center of the world." Sheba and Dedan and the merchants of Tarshish with all its villages will say to you, "Have you come to capture spoil? Have you assembled your company to seize plunder, to carry away silver and gold, to take away cattle and goods, to capture great spoil?"""

This is so fascinating to me. God basically says that on that specific day (that God ordained), Gog will contemplate the thoughts that come through his mind. These thoughts will cause him to "devise an evil plan," and in doing so, Gog will believe that he has come up with this idea to attack Israel all by himself. In truth, of course, God is the One who brought things together and simply dropped thoughts into Gog's head. It is also possible that God uses an evil spirit to put those thoughts into Gog's head. In either case, God credits Himself with it and blames Gog for following those instincts that these thoughts create.

Gog's plan seems reasonable to him. All of a sudden, he thinks about Israel (as he has probably done so many times before) and this time, it is as if he breaks through. This time, he asks himself the question, "Hey, why can't I simply go up against Israel and overcome them? Who is there to stop me?" Gog's answer to himself is that there is no one to stop him, and he certainly does not believe that Israel will be any real match for him and his armies.

Gog becomes emboldened because of "his" plan. He considers the unwalled villages of Israel. More than one commentator has indicated that this description sounds very much like a *kibbutz*. This is a communal village that normally has no walls around it. Groups of people live there and share what they grow among themselves.

The many unwalled villages – or kibbutzim – provide us another indication that the people of Israel are living securely. If they did not believe they were secure with the ability to overcome every threat, they would have built walls around their villages. They don't do this, instead leaving themselves quite vulnerable to an enemy invasion.

I know people who have wrought iron security bars on their doors and windows. It is a pain to unlock this door, then that one, then the wrought iron doors. They have special releases on the inside of their windows that will let them escape the flames in case of a house fire.

They feel very safe, but the reality is that it is quite possible they have exaggerated the threat, and because of the wrought iron bars, they feel as though their home is impenetrable. Maybe it isn't. Maybe it has provided them with a false sense of security.

The unwalled villages in Israel may not seem safe to us, but the people of Israel who live there understand the very real threat that they constantly live with, yet have decided to simply recognize that the threat is always there. Knowing that keeps them alert and therefore quite possibly far safer than the person who has triple locks on their doors and windows and then wrought iron bars on top of that.

In essence, though, Gog will decide that Israel *is* penetrable and he will believe he can do the job of taking Israel down. Gog decides to invade Israel because of spoil. We don't know what this spoil actually is that Gog wants to badly. The text simply says *silver, gold, cattle,* and *goods.* Those are pretty generic terms, and in point of fact, Israel today has quite a list of resources that are very valuable.

Oil has been recently discovered in Israel – enough oil that within a few years of production would make Israel totally self-sufficient. Beyond the oil reserves, great stores of natural gas and other resources have been found located within Israel's Land.

There are millions if not billions of dollars of valuable minerals within the Dead Sea. Extracting those minerals at this point is a very expensive project and would likely be cost prohibitive, but who knows what the future holds? At any rate, something of value will tempt Gog to pick up his weapons, gather his troops, and invade Israel for whatever he can capture to take home to his own nation. Spoils of war can be anything and it is obviously different in every war, every skirmish, and every disagreement. As far as Gog is concerned, he will be tempted to go into Israel to gain what he does not possess.

Once again, Gog believes that the idea to invade Israel comes from his own brain. He will become enamored with something that Israel has and will go after it. In all likelihood, this will involve Land as well, but we will not know for sure until it actually happens.

5

Gog Knows

Gog, the leader of the Northern Invasion that is introduced to readers in chapter 38 of Ezekiel, has a *thought*. That thought has a bad effect on him, as it leads him to *act*, by taking up weapons against Israel and their Land. This gets him in deep trouble with God. Up until that point, Gog is completely unaware of what God is up to, but of course God knows, because He *designed* it.

In Ezekiel 38:14-16 we read words that almost sound like Almighty God is taunting Gog. "*Therefore prophesy, son of man, and say to Gog, 'Thus says the Lord GOD, "On that day when My people Israel are living securely, will you not know it? You will come from your place out of the remote parts of the north, you and many peoples with you, all of them riding on horses, a great assembly and a mighty army; and you will come up against My people Israel like a cloud to cover the land. It shall come about in the last days that I will bring you against My land, so that the nations may know Me when I am sanctified through you before their eyes, O Gog."'"*

God repeats Himself here, and that's one of things I love about the Bible. God repeats Himself enough times so that there is no way to miss His point. Yet, sadly enough, people *still* miss it.

God sums up here, stating what we already know from previous chapters of Ezekiel, but He *adds* something, something that is extremely important for us to see and comprehend. This new bit of information is pertinent to the situation and it proves that God is behind this action that Gog believes is his own idea that came from the emptiness of his own head. Though Gog believes it is *his* idea to attack Israel because there is something *he* wants, the entire scenario is *God's* idea. The reason God chooses to do this is so that He will be *sanctified*, and he is going to use *Gog* to accomplish it!

Isn't that like God? He takes what we do as evil and makes it something that will ultimately bless and glorify His Name. There are many instances of this throughout the Bible, but let's just take a moment to look at one of them.

We're all familiar with Joseph and his brothers, the Patriarchs of Israel, sons of Jacob. They grew very jealous of Joseph and treated him badly. It all came to a head one day after Joseph had prophesied that they would all bow down before him (cf. Genesis 37). Of course, this did not go over well with Joseph's brothers. In fact, they hated him for it and decided they needed to do something about him. They were going to kill him, but Reuben persuaded them to not do that and instead put him in a well so that he could not escape. Reuben was planning on getting Joseph out later.

Before Reuben could help Joseph, the brothers decided to sell Joseph into slavery and then make it look like he had been killed by a wild boar. They even dipped Joseph's coat in blood to convince their ailing father that the story was true.

Joseph spent time in Potiphar's house and became the chief servant under whom all others worked. The problem was with Potiphar's wife, who just could not resist Joseph's good looks, apparently. She tried on several occasions to get Joseph to commit adultery with her, but he would have none of it. He did what he could to avoid her, but eventually she managed to corner him and when he tried to get away, she hung onto his outer cloak, leaving him running from the house naked.

Even though Joseph had done nothing wrong, he was imprisoned because Potiphar's wife accused Joseph and even had his clothing to "prove" her allegations. Joseph spent time in prison until he was needed by Pharaoh to interpret a dream – a dream about a coming famine. Joseph did interpret the dream, but he made sure he gave all the credit to God for that ability.

Eventually, Joseph was made the highest officer of the land, just under Pharaoh. With God's help and wisdom, Joseph made excellent decisions that worked well in Egypt, especially in the face of the major famine heading their way.

It was because of this famine that Joseph's brothers were sent down to Egypt by their father Jacob to buy grain, and it was there they met their brother for the first time in roughly 20 years since selling him into slavery. At first they were not aware of whom he really was because he was the second in command in all of Egypt. Beyond this, of course, time had passed, and Joseph certainly looked different and was dressed far differently than on that fateful day 20 years prior. Eventually, Joseph revealed his identity to them and they became understandably extremely afraid that Joseph would deal with them the way they dealt with him.

However, Joseph had learned a great deal and responded to their concerns with grace and love. He basically said that what they had meant for evil, God had meant for good (cf. Genesis 45). This is the mark of a man who had submitted himself to God over the years and had come to terms with what God had put him through. Because of it, God was fully glorified in and through Joseph. That is what God wants for all of His children, to use each of us to glorify *Himself*.

Though the outcome of the Northern Invasion is good as far as God is concerned, Gog will not willingly learn his lesson. He will not of his own volition submit Himself to God's rule. Everything Gog does toward Israel he does as if it came from his own brain. He credits himself with the idea to attack Israel, not realizing that what he means for evil, God means for good.

One of the wonderful things about God is the fact that He takes the time to tell us what He is going to do before He does it. Why does He do this? It is certainly not because He has to do it. He has no obligation to let us know of anything He does or will do.

He does it because He wants us to know that He is *trustworthy*. He tells us His plans so that when they come to fruition, we will be able to say, "*Praise the Lord! He has done it as He said He would!*" God actually stoops to our level, understanding our weak state and frame, and provides us with inside knowledge of His plans and purposes.

With respect to Gog, He (God) has given us His plan long before it happens. It is still yet future, but what do you think will happen for those who are familiar with this plan of His to use Gog to invade Israel? Those who know about this section of Ezekiel will either marvel or shut their mouths. They will marvel if they love Him, and they will shut their mouths if they want no part of Him. The former may try to say that this was all merely a *"coincidence,"* but they won't be able to convince themselves of that, try as they might. Ultimately, they will simply reject it out of hand, in spite of the fact that God has told them ahead of time what He will do.

God wants people to *know* Him. He doesn't just want people to know *about* Him. He wants all people to individually enter into relationship with Him, and that can only happen when people *believe* Him. If people refuse to know Him as He wishes to be known, they will be stubbornly left out of things and they will learn to know Him only as a God of *wrath*.

Verses 17 – 23 explain the details of God's reaction to Gog's attempted invasion of Israel. He tells us exactly how He will deal with Gog and his troops.

"'Thus says the Lord GOD, "Are you the one of whom I spoke in former days through My servants the prophets of Israel, who prophesied in those days for many years that I would bring you against them? It will come about on that day, when Gog comes against the land of Israel," declares the Lord GOD, "that My fury will mount up in My anger. In My zeal and in My blazing wrath I declare that on that day there will surely be a great earthquake in the land of Israel. The fish of the sea, the birds of the heavens, the beasts of the field, all the creeping things that creep on the earth, and all the men who are on the face of the earth will shake at My presence; the mountains also will be thrown down, the steep pathways will collapse and every wall will fall to the ground. I will call for a sword against him on all My mountains," declares the Lord GOD. "Every man's sword will be against his brother. With pestilence and with blood I will enter into judgment with him; and I will rain on him and on his troops, and on the many peoples who are with him, a torrential rain, with hailstones, fire and brimstone. I will magnify Myself, sanctify Myself, and make Myself known in the sight of many nations; and they will know that I am the LORD".'"

The images conjured up by the text are pretty intense. God reminds us that He has been speaking about Gog through many prophets and for many years. He does not want us to forget that this event will occur because God will make it happen and it *will* happen in the last days, the time during the last period of human history before Jesus returns. I believe those days are now. But let's look and see what God does in response to Gog's attempts to crush Israel and take spoils. When Gog moves against Israel, here's what happens:

1. God will become furious
2. God will cause a tremendously powerful earthquake to occur to be noticed by:
    a. The fish of the sea
    b. The birds of the heavens
    c. The beasts of the field
    d. All creeping things on the earth
    e. It will be felt the world over
3. The mountains will fall
4. Steep pathways will collapse into rubble
5. Every wall will fall to the ground
6. God will turn the tables on Gog, causing his armies to turn on one another
7. Pestilence (sickness and disease) will affect them
8. Torrential rains
9. Hailstones
10. Fire and brimstone

Wow, that is *some* picture we are getting there. Imagine it. God will become so angry that He will cause a very large earthquake to occur and it will affect *every living thing on earth* as well as inanimate things like mountains.

The earthquake is just the start, though, because God will then cause the troops to turn on each other and start fighting against one another. Wait a minute, weren't they there to attack Israel as one?

Yes, but God confuses them so that they begin to see one another as the enemy and react accordingly. This will undoubtedly be caused by great fear that runs through the entire army of Gog.

As if this is not enough, God is still not finished. Please notice that God says, *"It will come about on that day, when Gog comes against the land of Israel..."* and it is for that reason that God acts. Notice God is not acting because Gog has attacked the people of Israel yet. God is acting purely because Gog and his troops have dared to stampede God's *Land*. This is the reason for God's tremendous anger.

How *dare* Gog think he can simply waltz onto God's Land and do what he wants to do, taking what he thinks he can take! God is going to let Gog have it once and for all because by taking his troops and invading Israel, he has called God out. The Land of Israel is God's Land and He has had enough of people trying to divvy it up and break it apart. The world needs to know that God is the Owner of the Land in question and no one else.

Ultimately, God does this to spare the Land an assault from a godless enemy and to bring glory and honor to His Name. God will show Himself as Someone who is set apart from all of godless humanity and the godless system that moves throughout the world. It is governed by Satan, and for him it is the beginning of the end.

So upon seeing Gog and his forces move across His Land to the Mountains of Israel, God says *"ENOUGH!"* and causes the earthquake. That earthquake not only gets everyone's attention, but causes tremendous damage.

It is my opinion that this event will occur *prior* to the start of the Tribulation period. When? I have no clue, but I do believe it is a precursor to it. Because of this, I also believe that the resultant major earthquake will take out the two mosques that currently sit on the Temple Mount. After all, if this earthquake is powerful enough to bring down mountains and walls, knocking over the Dome of the Rock should be a piece of cake. Could this be the very thing that opens the door for Israel to build their third Temple? If it happens like this it could, but only time will tell when the actual event occurs.

With this earthquake, God is warming up. He then pulls out even more big guns. Pestilence, disease, and brother-fighting-brother become part of the event. But this is not the end. God then begins to send torrential rain, hailstones, fire and brimstone down onto the troops. Try to imagine the scene. A huge earthquake has occurred, leaving plenty of major damage and death in its wake. That is merely the *beginning*, though, as God really starts to cause havoc. The troops that are left (who have not been killed by the earthquake) become thoroughly confused and start fighting each other.

God then *joins* the fray and begins bombarding the enemy troops with major rainfall, hailstones, fire, and brimstone. I cannot imagine anyone surviving that onslaught, and with Gog dead, God rains down retribution on the area from which Gog came in the far north of Israel. God is making a statement here and He wants the world to see it and hear it. Israel does not raise a finger to help themselves. They won't need to because God does it.

In fact, at least temporarily, the world *will* recognize something supernatural in all of this. They will see that this could not have been a coincidence at all. It was too violent and the timing was too perfect. No, it must have been something beyond this world's powers. Will people turn to God because of it? Some might, but the majority will not, as we will eventually see.

6

Gog Pays the Price

Chapter 39 of Ezekiel shows us a picture of God dealing directly with Gog *after* He (God) routes the troops who were all set to fight under his command against Israel. No sooner do Gog and his troops set foot on the Mountains of Israel when God moves into high gear, creating a tremendously large earthquake, causing mass confusion, and slinging rain, hailstones, fire and brimstone at the invaders.

But God is not done with Gog *yet*. God has a point to make and He wants to be sure that Gog does not miss that point. The point is simple: God, *not* Gog, is in charge of world affairs, especially as those affairs relate to Israel.

"And you, son of man, prophesy against Gog and say, 'Thus says the Lord GOD, "Behold, I am against you, O Gog, prince of Rosh, Meshech and Tubal; and I will turn you around, drive you on, take you up from the remotest parts of the north and bring you against the mountains of Israel. I will strike your bow from your left hand and dash down your arrows from your right hand. You will fall on the mountains of Israel, you and all your troops and the peoples who are with you; I will give you as food to every kind of predatory bird and beast of the field. You will fall on the open field; for it is I who have spoken," declares the Lord GOD. "And I will send fire upon Magog and those who inhabit the coastlands in safety; and they will know that I am the LORD"'" (Ezekiel 39:1-6).

In these opening verses of chapter 39, God again states what He is planning on doing. With respect to Gog, He will:

1. Turn him around
2. Drive him on
3. Bring Gog up to the Mountains of Israel
4. Knock his weapons from his hand
5. Cause Gog to fall on the Mountains of Israel
6. Kill the troops
7. Cause the dead to become food for carrion and beasts
8. Pour out His wrath and retribution on Magog (the area of the world where Gog lived)

God does all of these things for the same purpose: so that the people will *know* that He is LORD. This is important, especially in our discussion of Israel today. What happens there is solely due to God's timing, goals, and will. Yet too many people look at Israel and say they do not deserve to have any Land in the Middle East. Too many from the world's society blame Israel for the ills and wars of the Middle East.

This is so absurd because Israel is not the ones who are constantly making threats. Israel is not vowing to destroy every last "Palestinian" or Arab in the region. Israel is not promoting violence against Syria, Jordan, Egypt, and other Middle Eastern territories and nations.

However, people wrongly believe that Israel does not deserve what she has, therefore the entire problem of the Middle East conflict is laid at Israel's feet. In truth, the *people* of Israel have very little to do with things.

So far, God has promised to restore the Land of Israel (cf. chapter 36), and then He will bring people back to that Land. Once He does that, He will begin the process of cleansing the Remnant from their sin through Jesus.

Then, to show the world that He (God) is fully in charge, He will cause a strong leader from the north of Israel to gather his troops, along with armies from allied nations, and they will attack Israel. However, as soon as those enemy armies step foot on the Mountains of Israel, God will rout them!

They will not even get to harm one Israeli. They simply will not get that far before God strikes them, and it is because they have stepped on God's Mountains of Israel. He is *that* jealous for His Land, not just the people.

The people of Israel today are godless. So are the people of many nations. This is not reason enough to cast them off. The overriding factor should be based on what God says He is doing in the Middle East, not whether or not we think the people of Israel are "righteous" or not. They are *not* righteous. They are sinners, fallen, and most are fully without salvation, just like their neighboring nations.

The one difference, though, between Israel and all other nations is what God has promised He will do with the Land of Israel and the nation of Israel. That is the only difference. That is what sets Israel (the Land and Remnant) aside for God to do His work.

This is the *only* reason why Israel (the Land *and* nation) should be supported, because God continues to carry out His plans for that Land and nation. There is nothing we can do to rationalize away our needed support for Israel. To do so – any way you slice it – opposes God and His purposes.

Again, *why* is God supporting the Land and nation of Israel? It is *solely* because He promised to do just that through Abraham. He is keeping His part of the bargain and in doing so will bring tremendous honor and glory to His Name. That is the *only* reason He is doing what He is doing with respect to Israel.

Does God not see what Israel does? Is He blind to the callousness of the people of Israel in their rejection of Him? Does He overlook their sin and rebellion? He no more overlooks Israel's callousness, sin, and rebellion than He does with any other person or nation. The reality, though, is that He has promised to turn that nation around, and He will do it!

We judge from outward appearances. We see what Israel is involved in and we condemn. We do not do the same thing with the Arab nations though, do we? We somehow hold Israel to a higher standard with more accountability. We blame them for the crucifixion of Jesus and say "God is *done* with Israel!" when that is not the truth.

Was God "done" with Adam and Eve? Did Jesus cast Peter permanently aside when He denied knowing Him? Does God cast YOU or ME aside when we sin? The reality is that there is *nothing* in Scripture that would attempt to show that God came to a point where He actually said, "*I've had it with Israel! They are dead to me!*" In fact, there are places in Scripture where God actually gave Israel a writ of divorce, but then *wooed* her back to Him (cf. Hosea). God did not create Israel only to destroy her, or simply to bring forth the Messiah, *then* destroy Israel. Yet this is what many theologians would have us believe. "The time of God's dealings with Israel is over. He is now focused only on the Church." You can only arrive at that conclusion through allegorization of the text, because the literal teaching and implication of Scripture is that God had a plan for Israel and He will follow it through until it is completely fulfilled.

In Ezekiel, God continues to declare things through the prophet Ezekiel. "*'My holy name I will make known in the midst of My people Israel; and I will not let My holy name be profaned anymore. And the nations will know that I am the LORD, the Holy One in Israel. Behold, it is coming and it shall be done,' declares the Lord GOD. 'That is the day of which I have spoken'*" (Ezekiel 39:7-8).

Notice that God specifically states that He will make His holy Name known in the midst of His people. Is that happening today through the Church? Yes, a bit here and a bit there. It can't happen through the Church because the visible Church is so filled with *tares*, who are people who *say* they are Christians, but live as if they are not. God is glorified through the *invisible* Church, but the world doesn't see that because they are too distracted by the visible Church.

People *will* notice when God glorifies His Name through Israel – both the Land and the Remnant. There will be no way for the world to ignore it! It will be way too obvious because of all that happens with respect to Israel.

How clear does God have to be here? He says that the *nations* will know that He is the *LORD, the Holy One in Israel*. Now, when will the final aspect of all of this ultimately occur? It will not fully take place until the Millennial Reign of Jesus when He will rule with a rod of iron, according to Revelation 2:27 and 19:15. In spite of His benevolence, His love toward humanity, and His kindness and compassion, there will be those who will try His patience. He will deal with it in an instant; thus the need to rule with a rod of iron.

God lists more specifics related to Israel after this attempted invasion takes place. *"'Then those who inhabit the cities of Israel will go out and make fires with the weapons and burn them, both shields and bucklers, bows and arrows, war clubs and spears, and for seven years they will make fires of them. They will not take wood from the field or gather firewood from the forests, for they will make fires with the weapons; and they will take the spoil of those who despoiled them and seize the plunder of those who plundered them,' declares the Lord GOD"* (Ezekiel 39:9-10).

This is interesting text. So far, we have learned that God will create within Gog the *desire* to attack Israel. He will follow through on his desire. The resultant attempted invasion will end in a massacre for Gog and his troops. We can see how this massacre actually winds up aiding Israel. Besides the fact that the world will see Israel in a completely different light, the people of Israel will gather the weaponry that is strewn across fields and use it for fuel for their fires. There will be enough here to not have to cut down a tree for seven years. That's obviously a good amount of weaponry.

Those living in Israel will also take plenty of spoils of war from the slain troops. These troops came to plunder Israel, and just as they did in the Six-Day War of 1967, Israel will turn the tables on their enemies.

I believe this time period of seven years also provides a big clue as to when this attempted invasion will occur. In my view, it must occur *before* the Tribulation begins, because the Tribulation is destined to last for seven years. If the invasion occurs after the start of the Tribulation, the end of the seven years may well run into the Millennial Kingdom. This is true if it takes place in the middle or the end of the Tribulation as well.

The only way these seven years could occur *without* impinging on any part of the Millennial Reign would be if the attempted invasion happened before the Tribulation starts.

Enter the Man of Sin?

I also believe that another reason can be seen here. Consider the fact that the world will see what has transpired. They will see Gog and his troops heading toward Israel. They will have front row seats to the event when those troops step foot on the Mountains of Israel. The world *will* notice these things, and whether or not they are willing to admit that something supernatural occurred to save Israel, they will at least outwardly have a new respect for Israel. This may be the perfect time for Antichrist to rise and enter the peace talk process.

After seeing such a defeat occur against such a massive number of troops, does anyone think that the world would want *another* shot at trying to invade and/or take over Israel? I don't believe it, and I even think that Arabs will begin to back down a bit from their anti-Semitic rhetoric. Then the Antichrist may waltz in, find a way to make peace (at least temporarily), and the Tribulation then *begins* with the opening of the first seal of Revelation 6.

You and I have seen videos of people rioting and running amok in the streets. We've seen the police and SWAT teams trying to handle the explosiveness of the crowds. Normally, it is only when force is used that rioters will back down. It tends to wake them up from their stupor and the blindness that has caused them to join the riot.

Snapped out of it, they begin to see things more clearly and realize that they are no match for the weapons of the riot police. Most begin to back down, while others continue rioting with their arrest as the result. Sometimes, it takes a rude awakening for people to be shocked out of their aberrant behavior.

I think that this is exactly what will happen in the Middle East, setting the stage for the Antichrist to be the hero of the world! Consider it. With the way the world is going now, national economies are being hit big time and there seems to be no end in sight. Famines, due to severe weather and natural disasters, are contributing to this situation. These things together are creating extremely untenable conditions for many nations, including the United States.

Nearly Russia's entire wheat crop was destroyed due to terrible weather conditions this past year. Russia is the second largest wheat exporter in the world, and because of the destruction, they have just recently decided to lift the ban on exporting of wheat — but it may be too little, too late for much of the world.

This type of shortage caused food prices to increase drastically. Besides this, gas prices have been on the rise as well, and since many countries including the U.S.A. are at the mercy of OPEC, there is little to do. These things continue to be harbingers of problems that will not go away on their own, and our leaders seem either unable or unwilling to stop the bleeding. In a global situation such as this, people become desperate to ensure that they have the resources they need to survive.

It is interesting to note that Israel is not experiencing these types of woes. In fact, with the recent oil and natural gas finds, it places Israel in an even better position to become completely autonomous with respect to needing to rely on other countries for their fuel needs. Unlike the United States and elsewhere, Israel cannot be held over a barrel because of it.

At the same time, it could very well be these resources in Israel that prompt certain leaders to take note of Israel at all. They may find themselves wanting what Israel has and may come to believe that going in and taking what they want is far easier and more productive than trying to buy them.

If things continue to escalate as they have been with food shortages, severe weather and natural disasters, the situation in the entire world will quickly become desperate for many. When people see that others have what they need, but cannot grow or buy, it may create the desire to take what they otherwise cannot have. Is it any different from the common criminal who seems to live by this rule?

So if our global economy gets to the point where it seems to be heading – a full-scale crash – the desperate times that would result from such a dire situation could very well create what is described in Ezekiel 37 as the Northern Invasion.

Once that event takes place and is met with the resultant wrath of God, I can see the world sitting back and trying to act as if they were not rooting for the enemy. At that point, the Arabs may well be prepared to at least pretend to want to "play nice," and the Antichrist may give them an offer they can't refuse.

The resultant offer will only *seem* to give Israel the upper hand, allowing them to rebuild the Temple – something most in Israel have yearned to happen for generations. All may seem lost for the Arabs, but in due time, Antichrist will show his true colors – not caring about Jews or Arabs – and will desecrate the rebuilt Temple, claiming himself to be god, just as we read in Daniel 9:27.

There is a plan and a purpose behind everything. What started out in the Middle East with the Garden of Eden, the eventual creation of the nation of Israel, and the life, death, and resurrection of Jesus, will also culminate in that same area of the world.

7

The Aftermath

This entire scene offers us a tremendous look into God's plans and purposes. He *will* bring them to fruition and the world *will* know that He is God. However, the world's memory is often short-lived, as we see repeatedly throughout the book of Revelation. There, though people wake to the fact that God is in the heavens, controlling all things, they quickly resort to their foolish, disobedient, godless ways.

Ezekiel 38-39 show God's perspective and bring us to the incontrovertible conclusion that God will have His day. As we continue in Ezekiel 39, God proceeds to tell us of His plans where Gog is concerned. *"'On that day I will give Gog a burial ground there in Israel, the valley of those who pass by east of the sea, and it will block off those who would pass by. So they will bury Gog there with all his horde, and they will call it the valley of Hamon-gog. For seven months the house of Israel will be burying them in order to cleanse the land. Even all the people of the land will bury them; and it will be to their renown on the day that I glorify Myself,' declares the Lord GOD. 'They will set apart men who will constantly pass through the land, burying those who were passing through, even those left on the surface of the ground, in order to cleanse it. At the end of seven months they will make a search. As those who pass through the land pass through and anyone sees a man's bone, then he will set up a marker by it until the buriers have buried it in the valley of Hamon-gog. And even the name of the city will be Hamonah. So they will cleanse the land'"* (Ezekiel 39:11-16).

God wants the world to realize and remember what He did to those who dared to attack Israel on His Land. There will be a burial ground for those who are killed, including Gog. This is another reason that I believe this cannot be referring to the final war we call Armageddon, which takes place at the end of the Tribulation. We read in Revelation 19:20, *"And the beast was seized, and with him the false prophet who performed the signs in his presence, by which he deceived those who had received the mark of the beast and those who worshiped his image;* **these two were thrown alive into the lake of fire** *which burns with brimstone"* (emphasis added).

Here we see that just after Jesus returns to earth, He destroys the power of the Antichrist and his armies. Then the beast (another name for the Antichrist) along with the False Prophet are taken into custody and literally thrown into the Lake of Fire *alive*. They are not buried, but simply transferred alive from this dimension to the dimension that contains the Lake of Fire. In fact, these two are the first inhabitants or prisoners of the Lake of Fire. Everyone else who will end up here is awaiting their sentencing in hell.

So we see that Gog and his massive army are not only defeated, but killed. Gog is buried here in the valley that becomes known as Hamon-gog (literally, *"Valley of the multitudes of Gog"*).[2]

Apparently, the task of burying all the dead will be massive, taking seven months to complete. It will become a full-time job for some, who will constantly move through the area marking places where skeletons or bones are found to be buried. This will actually continue after the seven months to ensure that all bones are located and buried in order for the Land to become cleansed.

There will be no doubt that God was the One who met Gog's force with force of His own. That force, predicated on His wrath, will leave nothing untouched, unscathed, or alive. All of Gog's ungodly forces will be decisively destroyed. Though it will be clear to the world that God literally involved Himself directly in human affairs, this is only a precursor to many more times that God's wrath will be clearly evidenced because of the hardness of people's hearts in this world.

With this next section of Scripture, God informs us *how* these dead bodies will be dealt with *before* they are buried. *"As for you, son of man, thus says the Lord GOD, 'Speak to every kind of bird and to every beast of the field, "Assemble and come, gather from every side to My sacrifice which I am going to sacrifice for you, as a great sacrifice on the mountains of Israel, that you may eat flesh and drink blood. You will eat the flesh of mighty men and drink the blood of the princes of the earth, as though they were rams, lambs, goats and bulls, all of them fatlings of Bashan. So you will eat fat until you are glutted, and drink blood until you are drunk, from My sacrifice which I have sacrificed for you. You will be glutted at My table with horses and charioteers, with mighty men and all the men of war," declares the Lord GOD'"* (Ezekiel 39:17-20).

---

[2] http://en.wikipedia.org/wiki/Valley_of_Hamon-Gog (accessed June 4, 2011)

Here, God shares with us through the prophet Ezekiel that He will gather carrion-eating birds of the air and beasts of the field. They will have so much meat to eat and blood to drink that they will become drunk with it.

Please notice that God considers His massacre of Gog and his troops a *sacrifice*. He states that He has done this as a sacrifice *for* these birds and beasts as He announces that this is their time to eat at His table.

Oh how I wish that people would turn to Him so that they could avoid becoming a sacrifice like this! Yet, it is due to their rebellious nature and self-service that they refuse to submit to the truth. The fact that we are aware of this truth is clear from Paul's teachings in Romans 1. We have no excuse. What could be plainer than what we read in Romans 1:18-23?

"For the wrath of God is revealed from heaven against all ungodliness and unrighteousness of men who suppress the truth in unrighteousness, because **that which is known about God is evident within them; for God made it evident to them**. *For since the creation of the world His invisible attributes, His eternal power and divine nature, have been clearly seen, being understood through what has been made, so that they are without excuse. For even though they knew God, they did not honor Him as God or give thanks, but they became futile in their speculations, and their foolish heart was darkened. Professing to be wise, they became fools, and exchanged the glory of the incorruptible God for an image in the form of corruptible man and of birds and four-footed animals and crawling creatures"* (emphasis added).

So, on one hand, all people are aware that something or Someone far higher than themselves has actually created. We did not evolve as many deliberately prefer to believe. God has given within each of us a hint of eternal knowledge that *can* lead us to eternal life. On the othere hand, most refuse that knowledge, making us culpable and guilty. At the same time, God will open the eyes of those who truly want to know Him.

I would implore you to seek God and His truth. He *will* open your eyes, allowing you to fully embrace that truth, entering into a life-changing relationship with Him that will continue for all eternity.

Gog and his military forces are those who have kept ignoring the basic truth that "God created," therefore God must exist. Done enough times, God will give *"them over to a depraved mind, to do those things which are not proper, being filled with all unrighteousness, wickedness, greed, evil; full of envy, murder, strife, deceit, malice; they are gossips, slanderers, haters of God, insolent, arrogant, boastful, inventors of evil, disobedient to parents, without understanding, untrustworthy, unloving, unmerciful; and although they know the ordinance of God, that those who practice such things are worthy of death, they not only do the same, but also give hearty approval to those who practice them"* (Romans 1:28b-32).

Those who spend their lives suppressing the truth that God has revealed are eventually *thrown* over to fulfill their own desires. This leads to a continual downward spiral as they move closer and closer to hell. Gog is a type of this in the extreme, and the final man of sin who will embody all of these traits and more will be the Antichrist.

In spite of all those who purpose to stand against God and His plans, nothing will keep those plans from being fulfilled. God will ensure that, and He will ensure that everyone knows that He is God. Ultimately, the final fulfillment of this will occur in the afterlife when people stand before Him at the Great White Throne Judgment (cf. Revelation 20:11-15). This is the final judgment that explains to people *why* they are going to be allowed to go to the Lake of Fire for all eternity. God does not *send* people there. He *allows* them to decide that for themselves.

"And I will set My glory among the nations; and all the nations will see My judgment which I have executed and My hand which I have laid on them. And the house of Israel will know that I am the LORD their God from that day onward. The nations will know that the house of Israel went into exile for their iniquity because they acted treacherously against Me, and I hid My face from them; so I gave them into the hand of their adversaries, and all of them fell by the sword. According to their uncleanness and according to their transgressions I dealt with them, and I hid My face from them" (Ezekiel 39:21-24).

In the final analysis, the world will fully come to realize that all that has happened to Israel has been due to their iniquity, sin, and rebellion. Because of it, God chased them out of the Land He had given them and allowed their adversaries to lord it over them. God caused this because of their tremendous sin. God hid His face from them and acted as though He could not hear them. This was for a *limited* amount of time, and the world will come to realize this when God restores Israel to the Land. God took the time not only to rebuke Israel on numerous occasions, but often went through the process of purging the rebels from the nation of Israel. This He had to do repeatedly because with each new generation, new people had to make their own decision about God. Think of how often Moses was criticized and condemned by many within the nation of Israel.

If God was speaking about the *invisible* (or true) Church here, it would not at all have the same impact on the world. Israel is the nation through which the Messiah Jesus came into the world. Israel is the nation that was the major part of God's plan of redemption. Israel is the nation that dragged God's Name through the muck. Their history is quite clear, and the Bible highlights the good, bad, and the idolatrous.

8

God Desires Restoration

God has always wanted to *restore*. We see this from the beginning when both Adam and Eve sinned, bringing a curse not only on themselves, but on the entire earth and all that inhabit it. Even though God had to judge the situation that Adam and Eve created, He immediately set out to restore all things, and He is still doing that.

The truth of His restorative nature is seen throughout the Old Testament as well as the New. The idea that He would somehow finally come to a point of absolute rejection of the nation of Israel goes against God's very nature. God is the God of restoration, and He wants all people to be restored to Him (cf Romans 8:19-22; 1 Corinthians 15:27-28; Colossians 1:20). Those who choose not to oblige choose for themselves an eternal abode that God did not originally create for them. He created it for the devil and his angels, not people (cf. Matthew 25:41). Since Adam's race – human beings – were created separately from all angelic hosts, and since God literally breathed life into Adam, setting him apart from the entire Creation and making Him in God's image, only humanity and things *under* humanity (including the entire animal kingdom and the earth) have the opportunity to be reconciled to God.

When Jesus died on the cross, His shed blood did not extend to the devil and the angels that fell. Jesus' death was for *humanity*. The curse that was set upon Creation was due only to man's sin. In reconciling man to God, it will then be possible that the things that came under the curse due to man's sin will also be reconciled.

We see the results of God's reconciling ability in the last portion of Ezekiel 39:25-29. *"Therefore thus says the Lord GOD, 'Now I will restore the fortunes of Jacob and have mercy on the whole house of Israel; and I will be jealous for My holy name. They will forget their disgrace and all their treachery which they [m]perpetrated against Me, when they live securely on their own land with no one to make them afraid. When I bring them back from the peoples and gather them from the lands of their enemies, then I shall be sanctified through them in the sight of the many nations. Then they will know that I am the LORD their God because I made them go into exile among the nations, and then gathered them again to their own land; and I will leave none of them there any longer. I will not hide My face from them any longer, for I will have poured out My Spirit on the house of Israel,' declares the Lord GOD."*

This is the final phase of God's restoration of Israel, both the Land and the nation. Having forced them to walk under the wrath as evidenced by His outstretched arm, He will then restore them through His mercy. He will have purged the rebels (once again) from that particular generation of Jewish people and will be left with a Remnant that is solely dedicated to Him at every turn. Never again will they sin against Him.

This is obviously referring to the time of the Millennial Reign when Jesus sets up His Kingdom on earth, reigning from His "father" David's throne. During this time, people will actually want to grab the robe of a Jewish person because they will want to be *associated* with Jews. This is a far different cry from today when the entire world seems bent on Israel's destruction.

God has protected Israel from complete annihilation and will make sure that He continues to keep a Remnant of believers for Himself so that they will go in and possess the Land during the Millennial Kingdom as they were originally meant to do.

At this point, God is wrapping up all the loose threads. Just as the Church – which is Jesus' Bride – will be the ones to gain what was lost through Adam and Eve, so will the nation of Israel finally possess the Land that God promised to Abraham centuries ago.

People today do not believe that, and I have read many convoluted arguments that are designed to "prove" that God is finally done with Israel and all blessings have been transferred to the Church. It is nonsense that ultimately labels God a liar. Of course, they do not see it that way at all because they believe that the Church was mentioned in the Old Testament. They get this because of the word that is used to describe a congregation in reference to Israel. That is hardly proof that the Church existed there, especially given the fact that the Church came into being on the day of Pentecost (cf. Acts 2). This was the birth of the Church and it did not replace Israel at all.

We are going to spend the remaining chapters dealing with aspects of Israel's restoration, among them being those found in Romans chapters 9 through 11. Here we will seek to understand just what Paul is talking about with reference to the future of Israel. Like most important sections of Scripture, these three chapters in Romans have been taken to mean a number of things. We'll present our views on these important chapters and you are free to decide for yourself if you think we are correct or not.

9

Will Israel Rise Again?

We will need to spend most of this chapter looking at the promises that God gave to Abraham. We will need also to determine the nature of those promises; are they *conditional* or *unconditional*? In other words, when God gave those promises to Abraham, was Abraham part of the covenantal agreement, in that he was required to do something which would uphold his end of the bargain? If so, then the Anti-Zionist's viewpoint certainly has merit.

If, on the other hand, the promises given to Abraham by God were *unconditional*, meaning nothing was required by Abraham in order for the covenant to stand and to be fulfilled, then the Anti-Zionist has a severe problem. The determination of who is correct – the Anti-Zionist or the Christian Zionist – stands or falls on whether or not God's promises were conditional or unconditional. It is truly that simple.

The Promises

The very first reference to any promise given to Abraham is found in Genesis 12:1-3. This is not only the first instance of the promises, but it is our second introduction to Abraham (called Abram at this point in the Scriptures). In chapter eleven of Genesis, his name is introduced to us. Let's see what the text says, shall we?

"Now the LORD said to Abram, 'Go forth from your country, and from your relatives and from your father's house, to the land which I will show you; And I will make you a great nation, and I will bless you, and make your name great; And so you shall be a blessing; And I will bless those who bless you, and the one who curses you I will curse and in you all the families of the earth will be blessed.'" (NASB)

Here, God comes directly to Abram and tells him a number of things:

1. Go to the land that He will show Abraham
2. God will make Abraham a great nation
3. God will bless Abraham
4. God will make Abraham's name great
5. Abraham will be a blessing
6. God will bless those who bless Abraham
7. God will curse those who curse Abraham
8. In (or through) Abraham all the families of the earth will be blessed

It all seems straightforward. Nothing appears to be hidden or cryptic. We are not talking about the writings of Nostradamus here. God's desire is that His Word should be plainly understood and that it should be consistent throughout. There does not seem to be any coded language here. God is making statements of "I will" to Abram. There appears to be nothing that Abram needs to do in order for God to keep His bargain with Abram. Oh wait! The very first sentence says "*Go forth from your country…*"

People argue that this part of the first sentence makes this a conditional covenant. In other words, God said "go" and as long as Abram went, things would be fine. If he failed to "go" then the agreement was off. Well, even if we agree (which we do not) that this directive telling Abram to "go" makes this a conditional covenant, it is clear from the following verses that Abram *did* go. The very next verse states: "*So Abram went forth as the LORD had spoken to him*" (Genesis 12:4; NASB). Okay, done. Abram went. Bargain kept. Covenant upheld. Now God is free to fulfill all that He said He would fulfill.

Here is some interesting information to consider: "*Why does the Torah mention all of the great rewards to Abram? Are they listed one by one in order to motivate Abram to respond in a positive way? No, these words do not serve as an enticement so that Abram will go. Abram will go because G-d said 'to go'.*"[3]

Abram "went" and now God can fulfill all eight items listed above. However, if we look closely at the verbiage here, God is *not* saying, "Abram, IF you will do this and then do this other thing, and keep my commandments, I will do these eight things in and through you." He says nothing of the kind. God is commanding Abram to "go" much like a parent would say "Son, mow the lawn today." Please do not try to tell me that the parent is entering into a conditional covenant with his son. A covenant does not even enter the picture. The parent – who clearly has authority over the child – is giving a command, and that parent expects the child to obey the command.

---

[3] Rabbi Yaakov Youlus, *Understanding the Language of G-D* (Jerusalem 2003), 34

This is what God is doing with Abram. He is telling Abram what to do. He is not saying "if" anywhere in the text. This is not a conditional covenant. It is all on God. It starts with God and it ends with God.

Let's say a father says to his son, "Son, mow the lawn today. After you mow the lawn, we will go to the sports store and get you a new pair of running shoes. This should make running track easier for you." Is this a covenant? Notice the verbiage. The parent is *not* saying "if" you do this, I will do this. The parent is giving a command, and *when* the son follows through on that command, then the next thing in line can occur, which in this case is going to the sports store for new running shoes. The parent is merely stating the order of events. It is a foregone conclusion because he knows that the son *will* carry through and mow the lawn. In the same way, God chose Abram because He already knew that Abram would comply by obeying.

Genesis 12:7
Moving a bit further into the chapter, we read these words: *"The LORD appeared to Abram and said, 'To your descendants I will give this land.' So he built an altar there to the LORD who had appeared to him"* (Genesis 12:7; NASB).

We know that Abram had obeyed God because the text states that. As he traveled, he eventually came to the area called Shechem. The text also tells us that people called Canaanites already lived in that area (cf. v. 6). It was at this point that God literally appeared to Abram and made the statement to him in verse seven. What was Abram's response? He built an altar to the Lord there. This was done as a form of worship. Notice that Abram says nothing. He is simply on the receiving end of the Lord's statement. God tells Abram to go to a land that He will show him. Abram begins moving and when he gets to that land area, God appears and says, *"This is the land I was talking about. This is the land that I will give to your descendants."* So far, Abram has done nothing to earn anything. He has done nothing that would indicate that he was required to do anything to uphold his end of any bargain. As stated, if we argue that Abram was required to "go" then it is obvious that he did go. If that was the requirement, then he fulfilled it. There was absolutely nothing else he was required to do. Nothing. By all counts, this was an unconditional covenant in which God was the only party with any requirements at all. Notice also that God placed those requirements on Himself.

Genesis 15

The next event in the continuing saga of Abram's dealings with God is found in chapter fifteen of Genesis. Here God again confirms His covenant with Abram. As we read through chapter fifteen, we see nothing that even remotely appears to be a conditional covenant.

Chapter fifteen of Genesis is an extremely interesting chapter. The reader would do well to take the time right now to read through it a few times before moving on. Here, God comes to Abram, again pointing out aspects of the covenant He is making with Abram.

In the previous chapter – fourteen – Abram has just returned from victoriously rescuing his nephew Lot. As he was returning, Abram met the King of Salem, named Melchizedek, who the text states was "*a priest of God Most High*" (Genesis 14:18; NASB). This was an extremely unusual office for a king. As a rule, a person was either a king or a priest, but not both. Interestingly enough, God had not even instituted the priestly line yet for Israel. King Melchizedek blessed Abram and then Abram did something equally unusual, by giving Melchizedek a tithe (cf. 14:20).

Many commentators believe that Melchizedek is a type of Christ, and there are many good reasons to accept this rationale. Certainly, it is understood that Melchizedek, as priest, presents bread and wine, which remind us of the last supper of Christ with His apostles as He instituted this sacrament just prior to His crucifixion.

The writer of Hebrews also refers to the "order of Melchizedek" as being royal and unending (cf. Hebrews 6:20). This of course compares with Christ's unending High Priesthood on behalf of all believers.

Later in chapter fifteen, after God Himself has promised Abram an heir, He takes Abram outside and shows him the heavens. God states, *"'Now look toward the heavens, and count the stars, if you are able to count them.' And He said to him, 'So shall your descendants be'"* (Genesis 15:5; NASB). God is making a promise to Abram that his descendents will be so vast, they will not be able to be numbered. Considering the fact that Abram was at this point without an heir, this is certainly saying a great deal.

A few verses later, God recounts to Abram what He has already done with and for him when He states, *"I am the LORD who brought you out of Ur of the Chaldeans, to give you this land to possess it"* (Genesis 15:7; NASB). Please do not miss what God is saying. He is crediting Himself with taking Abram out of UR. He gives no credit to Abram at all. So much for a conditional covenant. God is fully in command here, leaving nothing to chance. God took Abram out of UR and He *will* get him to the land that his descendents will possess. It is all in God's hands. No responsibility for any of it rests upon Abram at all.

The next verse is an extremely important verse, making a very solid point, which should not be missed or glossed over. It says, *"Then he believed in the LORD; and He reckoned it to him as righteousness"* (Genesis 15:6; NASB). Abram *believed* the Lord, and at that moment God *reckoned* or *applied to his account* God's righteousness. It was at that moment that Abram received salvation! It is the exact same salvation that I received, and you receive (if you are a Christian), and every other Christian receives. It is the salvation that is based on faith and when that faith is evidenced, God then imputes to us Christ's righteousness, removing our *unrighteousness* forever.

Allen P. Ross comments, *"Central to the entire chapter is the report of Abram's belief in the Lord and the Lord's crediting him with righteousness (v. 6). This statement is the chapter's explanation of Abram's obedience and the solution for Abram's tensions. Abram received the specific word from God as well as the solemn guarantee that his seed would inherit the land; but the fulfillment of those promises seemed to lag far behind – he had no son, and then he learned that there would be a longer delay when his descendants would be oppressed for four hundred years in a foreign land. It would take faith to wait for the promises; but faith was what God was looking for, and faith made Abraham acceptable to God."*[4]

Abram's New Birth

It is patently clear then that it was Abram's *faith* which allowed God to grant him salvation. It was nothing that Abram did to secure it on his own. It was faith alone.

From that point onward, just as with Abram, for the person who, through faith in Jesus' atoning work, embraces salvation, God sees Christ's righteousness when He looks at us. He no longer sees our unrighteousness. One might ask how God can do this since Christ had not yet died on Calvary's cross. Very simply, God merely looked "forward" (from man's perspective) to that point when Christ would die and "borrowed" (if you will) or credited Christ's righteousness to Abram's account.

The cross of Christ is always before God, since God exists outside of our time dimension. He sees all of time, all at once. Whether a man lives before the cross or after has no bearing on the situation. From God's perspective, it is always an *accomplished event,* and as such, the righteousness of Christ already existed for imputation.

---

[4] Allen P. Ross *Creation & Blessing* (Grand Rapids Baker Academic 1998), 305

The Old Testament saint was always saved the same way anyone is saved today: through the shed blood of Christ on the cross and man's faith in that finished work. It was never *grace plus works* in the Old Testament vs. *grace alone* in the New Testament. It is *all* grace alone. The good works that anyone does (whether from the Old Testament, the New Testament, or today) all *stem* from the new life that comes into fruition once salvation is received. Those good works are *not* done to earn salvation. They are there as a proof that the new life exists within the individual. James makes this clear, as do John and Paul and other writers of the New Testament epistles.

Of course, Abram's next question is a logical one. He wants to know how all of this will be, since he does not even have an heir. How will he be able to *possess* the land that God has promised to him with no visible descendants? The Lord's answer comes in the form of another command in verses nine through seventeen of chapter fifteen.

"9-[God] said to him, 'Bring me a heifer three years old, a female goat three years old, a ram three years old, a turtledove, and a young pigeon.' 10-And he brought him all these, cut them in half, and laid each half over against the other. But he did not cut the birds in half. 11-And when birds of prey came down on the carcasses, Abram drove them away.

"12-As the sun was going down, a deep sleep fell on Abram. And behold, dreadful and great darkness fell upon him. 13-Then the LORD said to Abram, 'Know for certain that your offspring will be sojourners in a land that is not theirs and will be servants there, and they will be afflicted for four hundred years. 14-But I will bring judgment on the nation that they serve, and afterward they shall come out with great possessions. 15-As for yourself, you shall go to your fathers in peace; you shall be buried in a good old age. 16-And they shall come back here in the fourth generation, for the iniquity of the Amorites is not yet complete.'

"17-When the sun had gone down and it was dark, behold, a smoking fire pot and a flaming torch passed between these pieces. 18-On that day the LORD made a covenant with Abram, saying, 'To your offspring I give this land, from the river of Egypt to the great river, the river Euphrates, 19-the land of the Kenites, the Kenizzites, the Kadmonites, 20-the Hittites, the Perizzites, the Rephaim, 21-the Amorites, the Canaanites, the Girgashites and the Jebusites.'"

There are some extremely important things happening in the text above, and we need to focus on them. The verse numbering has been left in, in order for the reader to locate the verse easier. As we shine the light on this passage, we will have a better picture of the exact nature of the covenant God is making with Abram.

The promises contained in Genesis 15:5 are equally important, and the verification of them is the impetus for what occurs next. God is reminding Abram of the original promise, the one we read in Genesis 12:1-3.

Some commentators point out that these promises God made to Abram were not for *this earth* but actually for the next life. This view turns God's literal promises into allegories, which take on a meaning that is not there in the text. Certainly, on one hand, if the fulfillment of these promises was only for the *afterlife*, then Abram had absolutely no reason to worry. Nevertheless, Abram was concerned, and it caused tension for him which he hoped God would dispel.

In response to whether the promises of God were for *this* life or the *next* one, R' Moshe Ben Nachman (also known as Ramban or Nachmanides) comments on this question. He states, *"Now, it never entered [Abraham's] mind that this promise of great reward will be in the World to Come, (1) for this does not require a promise, for every person who serves God will find' [eternal] life before Him. In this world, however, there are religious people to whom there befalls [recompense] like the deeds of the wicked; therefore, one requires an assurance. (2) Furthermore, God's warning [your reward is] very great – implied that he would merit to eat at two tables, with all the material goodness that befits completely the righteous people, with no punishment for sins at all. (3) Furthermore, [God's] assurance was a response in kind to what [Abraham] feared. After Abraham made this request, [God] repeated and explained His promise to [Abraham], that he need not fear this childlessness either, for He will make his offspring as numerous as the stars of the heavens (v. 5)."*[5]

Beginning in verse nine of chapter fifteen, we read God's instructions to Abram. He is told to bring a heifer, a female goat and a ram, all being three years old. God also tells him to bring a turtledove and a pigeon. Abram obtains these requested animals and then cuts each of them (except the birds) in half. He then laid each half over against the other.

Apparently, after this Abram simply waited, because the text tells us that birds of prey came to try to eat the dead animals, but Abram drove them away. It appears as though Abram was waiting for the sun to go down (v. 12). As it began to grow dark, out of the blue, a deep sleep falls upon Abram.

While Abram slept, a terrible, palpable darkness came upon him. At this point, God speaks and tells Abram:

- His offspring *will* live in a land that is not theirs, and they will be servants there
- His offspring will be afflicted for four hundred years
- God will judge the nation they serve
- His offspring will eventually leave with great possessions

So, God reaffirms the promise to Abram. He also provides more elucidation as well, providing details He had not provided before.

---

[5] The Torah: With Ramban's Commentary, ArtScroll Series (Mesorah Publications, Ltd 2004), 341-342

Beginning in verse seventeen, we see that the mood changes. We are told that the sun had gone down, it had become completely dark, and then an extremely interesting and unusual event took place. A smoking fire pot along with a flaming torch passed over the altar and *between* the severed pieces of animals. We then read that God spoke and promised Abram that He (God) would give this land to Abram's offspring. God then outlines the boundaries for Abram.

Even though Abram was apparently deep in sleep, God spoke to him in a dream, which was the reason Abram sensed "dreadful and great darkness." So although Abram could not physically participate in the ceremony, he could "watch" it from deep within sleep and hear what God was telling him.

10

Attacks on Scripture

The amount of misinformation available today on many subjects related to Christianity is astounding, but not surprising. It makes sense if we stop to consider the fact that Satan, our enemy, is out to *undo* whatever God *does*, or to try to keep God's will from occurring. Satan often attempts to thwart God's work even before God completes it. While he is certainly *not* all-knowing, Satan without doubt knows the Bible, *learning* from what God reveals to His children. His attempts to disrupt or destroy God's plans always fall flat, of course, but at times, there are a great deal of storm-laden winds and noise surrounding his efforts to destroy God's Church.

From all of this activity, it would be easy to believe that Satan is winning, or at least gaining a foothold, but the truth is that he is absolutely *not* winning. In fact, his defeat was put on display at the cross, through Christ's death and resurrection. Satan's defeat is assured and final. He is, however, *allowed* to do what God permits him to do, until his defeat is made actual at a predetermined point in our future.

Satan's Methods

One of the things Satan specializes in is creating disunity within the visible Church. This is most frequently accomplished through

1) *A confusion or lack of understanding regarding biblical doctrine,*
2) *An overemphasis on certain aspects of doctrine, or*
3) *The sensationalizing of individual doctrines.*

These three things, coupled with a lack of patience or maturity within the individual, can easily set Christians against one another. The enemy can easily use this situation to create compromise, disunity, hatred, and even condemnation.

In many cases, the nature of the debate turns into a religious battlefield, complete with name-calling. Results are often seen in the form of casualties on both sides. The fallout is often arrogance, anger, hatred, lack of forgiveness and more.

To be clear, there are doctrines that *are* worth fighting for, and the Christian should always be willing and *able* to defend them. Doctrines such as the gospel of Jesus Christ (e.g. salvation by God's grace, through faith in Christ's work on the cross), His deity, the Trinity, the reality of hell, and many other areas of theology should never be given any ground by a Christian. Yet, at the same time, it is just as important to know *when* to stop arguing about it. Satan would love nothing more than for those within the visible Church to be in constant debate about some theological subject. If those within the visible Church are consistently embroiled in religious debate, they are not *evangelizing*, nor are they *living* for Christ. They are living to *win* the debate.

Not long ago, an individual and I had been discussing (and disagreeing about) an aspect of Eschatology, when he pointedly indicated that he had "never lost a debate!" He further mentioned a friend of his who also "never lost a debate." I asked him who or what was the determining factor for deciding the winner. He had no direct response, but simply reiterated what he had just stated, and then changed the subject. It seems clear enough from Scripture that Jesus never debated. He stated.

Being ready with a biblical response is absolutely necessary. Too many Christians do not know *what* they believe, or *why* they believe it. But beating someone over the head with a Bible until they "get it" usually accomplishes nothing good. Beyond this, that approach normally creates ill feelings and arrogance.

A Perfect Example
The following quote is from someone who has an interesting blog page on the 'Net, to say the least. She considers *herself* an authentic Christian, and it is interesting to read what she says about those she labels Christian Zionists (due to their support for Israel).

> *"'Fundamentalist Christians' (sometimes called 'Fundies') are, characteristically, Zionist, not Christian. In practice, they reject the teaching of Jesus in the New Testament: that each of us is equally precious in the eyes of the Lord. Instead, they live in the world of the Old Testament, where a mean-spirited Jehovah played favorites with his children, giving some (now called 'Jews') the OK to commit unspeakable acts of barbarism upon the*

> others ('Gentiles'). Read the Book of Joshua if you don't believe this.
>
> "Zionist Fundies will do anything for Israel and 'the Jews,' whom they worship as God or God's little brother. They are only too happy to be the Jews' slaves, and insist we all join in their bondage. Certainly their beliefs are anti-Christian.
>
> "More to the point: Zionist 'Christians' are **traitors to America**. Along with Jews, they wave the American flag, urging us to spill the blood of any who stand in the way of Israeli ambition. Along with Jews, Zionist Christians scream loudest for Arab blood, even though all rational analysis shouts that Israel and Israeli agents in America were responsible for 9-11. Along with Jews, Zionist Christians would happily have America spill its own blood to help Israel realize its ambitions."[6] (emphasis added)

The tragedy of Carol A. Valentine's caustic (and untrue) comments quoted above are obvious to anyone who understands that God's completed will for Israel is yet to be fulfilled. A number of things become evident immediately upon reading her malicious rhetoric. Apparently, she sees Jehovah as "mean-spirited" based on her understanding of the Old Testament and why God worked the way He worked. Apart from that and the fact that she has made sweeping generalizations, which rest on her opinion only, she has in one swell swoop decided that Christian Zionists are:

- "Fundies" (a negative slur against Fundamentalism)
- *Not* Christian
- Those who reject Christ's teaching and authority
- Those who do not love all people equally
- Unable to understand Scripture (reference to Joshua)
- Mean-spirited

---

[6] http://www.public-action.com/911/chrzion.html

- Worshippers of Jewish individuals
- Willing to be in bondage to Jews
- Anti-Christian in their beliefs
- Traitors to America
- Cheerleaders for Israel's aggressive acts against the Arabs
- Warmongers for Israel's cause

Anti-Semitism
The unavoidable conclusion gleaned from her comments is readily seen as anti-Semitism. This is one of the clearest signs that an individual has misunderstood the Bible and God's purposes. Beyond her anti-Semitism, it is also clear that Valentine fails to understand *why* He has chosen to do things the way He has chosen to do them.

Understandably, no one likes to hear that they may, in fact, be guilty of harboring racist attitudes towards another group. It should also be noted that not all Covenant or Replacement Theologians or Preterists are anti-Semitic. However, one is too many.

While Valentine and folks like her are quick to point out what *they* believe to be racism *against* Arabs by those who support Israel, she seems completely blind to her own anti-Semitism and the degree to which it exists. Becoming far too common today, this tragedy cannot be overlooked. Anti-Semitism can occur when people do not use a correct hermeneutical approach in their Bible study. This, in turn, often leads to a faulty interpretation of Scripture.

The common complaint among those who oppose Israel's statehood has to do with how our taxes are used in this country. Anti-Zionists are upset over the fact that a large chunk of tax dollars goes to support Israel militarily and financially. Even so, this is not the only place public tax dollars are spent. While the taxes I pay go to support Israel, my taxes are also currently used for many other things which I do not morally support:

- Abortion
- Subsidizing big business
- Too many government freebie programs
- Stem cell research, and many other things!

There are many businesses that I would prefer not to have any dealings with, solely because of the issues and/or groups they support. If I were to realistically stop shopping at all the places I object to, I would have nowhere to shop at all.

My Tax Dollars
While the odd case of so-called "Christians" shooting abortion doctors, blowing up their buildings, or committing other atrocities exists, those events are very rare. That is obviously *not* the way to handle a disagreement over policy and laws of this land.

If I had my druthers, my taxes would go *only* where I wanted them to go. It is likely that most Americans feel that way (at least the ones who honestly report and pay their taxes).

Their Tax Dollars
Anti-Zionists do not like their tax dollars being used to support Israel's "aggression." To them, the fault lies with *Israel* for the conflict which exists in the Middle East. To support Israel goes against the grain of practical (and they would say, *biblical*) peace. However, in reality, that area of the world has been a continual hotbed of war, corruption, and aggression (and all the rest that goes with it) nearly since the beginning of time.

Valentine expresses her sentiments with seeming spite, anger, contempt and indignation. Though she insists *"that each of us is equally precious in the eyes of the Lord,"* it would appear that this *preciousness* she speaks of does not extend to those who support Israel, or for that matter, to the Jewish people either. Valentine's view of God's preciousness is myopic, offered only to Arab individuals or those who *support* them. This is troublesome to say the least.

What we learn from people who believe as Valentine does is that words and motives are directly related to unacknowledged *Anti-Semitism*. This would no doubt be denied, but words like Valentine's seem clear enough.

Warfare in the Spiritual Realm
Although Paul clearly points out that we are not wrestling against flesh and blood, but against powers and principalities (cf. Ephesians 6:12ff), Anti-Zionists have decided that Paul is wrong, and that we *are,* in fact, wrestling against other people. We see this because of the fact that Anti-Zionists direct poison-filled words at Christian Zionists everywhere.

While Valentine condemns the Christian Zionist as evil, she remains completely confident in her *own* standing before God. It is clear, though, that her words and demeanor call her own Christian testimony into question. Sadly, she seems not in the least concerned.

Christ's Teachings
Anti-Zionists are quick to point to Christ's teachings in the New Testament. They do this while accusing the Christian Zionist of living in the *Old* Testament and ignoring the teachings of Christ in the process. It seems that those within the Anti-Zionism camp look *only* to Christ's *direct* teachings, largely ignoring Paul and other writers of the New Testament epistles. The numerous promises of God's *to* Israel, which have been recorded in the Old Testament, are also ignored.

With respect to the Old Testament, Anti-Zionists have a unique outlook. They point out that Christ Himself came to fulfill the Law (OT). Since He fulfilled it, then *all* of it has been fulfilled.

When interpreting Scripture, one of the most important rules to observe is the rule of *context*. This is used daily in all forms of communication, without a second thought. It is the context that, in many ways, largely provides meaning to the thoughts that are written or voiced. If all words had only *one* meaning each, context would not be so important, for obvious reasons. Since that is *not* the case, however, context becomes an extremely important tool in the interpretative process.

Referring again to Alan Nairne, he comments on the interpretive process as it relates to salvation:

> *"Salvation-history is continuous from the first promise of redemption given to Adam and Eve following the sin which they brought into the human race. This promise decreed warfare, which would take place between the seed of the serpent and the seed of the woman who would crush the head of the serpent (Gen.3:15). Whilst this warfare would in each generation be played out on the stage of human history, the prophecy related primarily to THE SEED, who is Jesus, the Son of God. Paul makes this clear in the Galatian epistle (3:16) that although Abraham received covenant promises concerning his seed, the promise was not to Abraham's 'seeds', the many, but to one SEED, who is Christ. Prophecy largely terminates upon HIM. It is only in Christ we inherit these redemptive promises. Rev.19:10 is to a similar effect - '...the testimony of Jesus is the spirit of prophecy.' As Paul states, 'Christ is the end of the law unto righteousness to everyone that believes.' Rom.10:4. Even when the church was seen afar off in the OT prophecies (Eph.3:5), its purpose was that '...unto him be glory in the church by Christ Jesus throughout all ages, world without end. Amen' (Eph.3:21). And to the Colossians '...he is the head of the body, the church: ....that in all things he might have the preeminence.' (Col.1:18).*

> *"In postulating a millennial kingdom, with Jewish dominance, sacrifices, temple, priesthood, etc., there is a subtle shift of emphasis away from Christ's preeminence, to say nothing of it being in plain contradiction to the messages of Galatians and Hebrews, as I hope we shall see."*[7]

Unfortunately, Nairne seems to miss the point when He speaks of the Millennial Kingdom. He sees it as Jewish *dominance* and claims there is a "subtle shift" *away* from Jesus. This is simply not true. Is he forgetting that Jesus Himself is *the* Ruler during that period? The Temple, the newly redesigned sacrificial system all points to Jesus Christ. The fact that He is also Jewish in heritage serves only to emphasize this point. Jesus is completely *dominant* during the Millennium Kingdom. As Absolute Ruler of the *entire world*, and stationed in Jerusalem, how is the point of the Millennium *not* showcasing Jesus as the dominant theme of this period?

Everything about the Millennial Kingdom points *to* Jesus, not away from Him. Let's consider the facts of the Millennium:

- The Jewish Remnant will possess the Land, as God's promises are ultimately fulfilled during this period
- Jesus will reign worldwide, as Absolute Ruler, from Jerusalem
- As Absolute Ruler, Jesus will
    - Establish absolute justice
    - Rule with a rod of iron because the sin nature is resident in humans who live and are born during this time
- Jesus will eradicate problems immediately as they arise
- Jesus will oversee the Temple and all that takes place within it, including the sacrifices
- Jesus will immediately quell Satan's last attempt to overthrow Him

---

[7] http://www.apocalipsis.org/Israel.htm

In all areas, Jesus is supreme, and He will be seen as that. That the Jewish Remnant will actually possess the Land as promised points to God's truthfulness. The fact of the Temple points to the fulfillment of Jesus regarding the Law. The newly redesigned sacrificial system serves to remind people the importance of Jesus' sacrifice. It also provides a way for human beings who are *born* during the Millennial Kingdom to come to understand the entire process of the sacrifices as related to Jesus.

One of the major difficulties for people when they consider the Millennial Kingdom is what they seem to forget. Since human beings *enter* the Millennial age having survived the Great Tribulation, and other human beings will be born during that time, they will have a sin nature. Those born during the Millennium will have no knowledge of the need for salvation. They will certainly not be aware of the fact that Jesus purchased this salvation on Calvary's cross. Until these things are explained to them, they will see no need for any of it. They will see the sacrificial system (which is somewhat different than the Old Testament system), and they will hopefully realize that they need to turn their life over to Jesus as much as everyone else does. Their need to receive Christ as Savior *then* will be just as necessary as it is *today*.

Think about what it will be like for people born *during* that time. Unlike our life, they will *see* Christ. They will *hear* Him. They will *experience* life under His physical reign. We do not. While He reigns from His Father's throne now, during the Millennium He will reign physically from His earthly "father's" (David's) throne, as was prophesied centuries ago (cf. Revelation 20).

The people who come into the world during that period will have absolutely *nothing* to compare it with, and it will be unlikely for them to comprehend what life is like for us now. They will see Christ in all His glory, reigning supremely, as no one else ever has or ever will.

Sin committed by those with a sin nature (all human beings who either go into the Millennium alive *after* the Tribulation, or those born *during* the Millennium), while enjoying life in the Millennium will cause a certain amount of strife between people and nations. However, Christ – who will rule with a rod of iron because of the sin nature – will deal with problems immediately as they occur. Though not perfect, the Millennial Kingdom will be the closest thing to perfection this side of the Eternal Order of the future, which *will* be perfect.

Nairne also seems to miss the full ramifications of what is taught in both Galatians and Hebrews with respect to the fullness of our salvation experience. In actuality, the truth of these two epistles is yet *future*, and will not become the fully realized actual experience of all the redeemed until the Eternal Order.

As long as human beings (even redeemed ones), live on earth, the full breadth of these spiritual realities will not be the experience of redeemed human beings. While Paul tells us that this is the natural experience of all those who – through death or (future) Rapture – live in the heavenly realm, it does not, nor will not, exist in all its fullness experientially for those of us who, though redeemed, *remain* in our corrupted human bodies. This is extremely important and *impossible* to under emphasize.

Following the Millennial Kingdom, the final resurrection and Great White Throne judgment occur, followed by a complete and absolute destruction of this present earth and the heavens which surround it. Following Christ's destruction of the earth and heavens He will make a completely *new* earth, with new heavens surrounding it. At that point, the full extent of everything that Paul speaks of in Galatians, along with the truths taught in Hebrews, will *become* the norm for *everyone*.

Anti-Zionist Says: No Grace for the Jew or Christian Zionist
It would also appear that while Valentine accuses the Christian Zionist of *rejecting* Christ's teachings, she is herself rejecting the very same teachings. Jesus gave commands to *turn the other cheek, be kind to those who despitefully use you, forgive over and over and then again*, and more beyond, but these are only *selectively* followed, as we will see.

In Valentine's mind, it becomes necessary to castigate individuals whom *she* believes do not at all fall *under* the grace of Christ. Again, while she *states* that we are all precious to God, there is absolutely no evidence that she believes that Jews and Christian Zionists come under the banner of God's grace and preciousness.

It would be best to try to determine what Christian Zionism is at its root. What does it stand for? Is it truly possible to be a Christian *and* a Zionist as well, or are these terms mutually exclusive, from a biblical point of view?

As noted in the *Prologue*, Christian Zionism believes that God created Israel to be a *special* people to Him. That nation was created for a special purpose. Israel was brought into being to be *His* nation. They were meant to be the light of the world, shining the truth of God's Word to the nations around them, ultimately pointing to the Messiah, Jesus Christ.

Jehovah's Wife
We all know that due to Israel's unbelief, the nation consistently failed in its relationship with God. Israel as depicted as the wife of Jehovah in the Old Testament (*already* married to Jehovah) was a wife who *always* looked for greener pastures. There are many instances in Scripture where God speaks to Israel *as though* already married.

One such example is found in Jeremiah 3:14, which states, "*'Return, O backsliding children,' says the LORD; **'for I am married to you**. I will take you, one from a city and two from a family, and I will bring you to Zion'*" (NKJV; emphasis added).

In the book of Hosea, the prophet is told by God to marry a specific woman. This particular woman eventually becomes a harlot, or prostitute, and God wanted Israel to recognize herself in the symbolism of that narrative.

When Temporary Becomes Permanent

There were times in the Old Testament in which God *temporarily* rejected Israel because of her unfaithfulness. He set her aside, often ignoring her for hundreds of years at a time. There were a number of captivities by foreign nations who took the people of Israel captive, or slaughtered them, or a mix of both. It was only after a time of renewal within the nation of Israel that God saw fit to release them from their captivity.

It is extremely important to note, however, that God *never* once rejected them *with finality and permanence*. It is equally significant to recognize that God has always dealt with Israel as a corporate body. While He chooses specific individuals throughout Israel's history in the Old Testament, He did so to lead and/or unite the entire nation of Israel.

Normally, what happened to one person in the nation happened to the entire nation. Through intercessory prayer, God would often refrain from eliminating the nation as a whole, opting instead to deal with those specific individuals who had rebelled. Yet, often the entire nation suffered consequences of one person's sin.

God Always Deals with Israel as One Nation

The wandering in the wilderness for forty years is a perfect example of this. Most of us are familiar with the event that brought God's judgment on the nation, as recorded in the book of Numbers, chapters thirteen and fourteen.

Moses had sent the twelve spies into the land and when they returned, they gave their report. Ten of the spies were fearful and unconvinced that God would provide the victory over the people in Canaan. Two of the spies – Joshua and Caleb – knew beyond doubt that God *could* and *would provide* the victory. The people of the nation, however, chose to believe the ten naysayers, not Joshua and Caleb. In fact, there was nearly a riot in which the people called for the death of Moses (cf. Numbers 14)!

This resulted in God stating to Moses that He wanted to wipe Israel out, which prompted Moses to intercede on Israel's behalf. Because of this, God is said to have *relented*. Nevertheless, let's be clear here. God was *not* going to wipe them out at all. He wanted Moses to act as their intercessor, which would bless *him*, as well as the people of Israel. God did *not* change His mind. When we speak of God relenting, the text is relating something in human terms so that we grasp it.

Even though God "relented," judgment still came, with the entire nation forced to wander in the wilderness for forty years. This was done so that every last man from that particular generation above a certain age would die in the wilderness. They had refused to believe that God could give them victory, in spite of the many miracles that He had shown them day in and day out. God had decided He was finished with those particular rebels. Interestingly enough, Paul is really commenting on Jewish individuals *like* this in the book of Romans (cf. Romans 11). When he refers to spiritual Jews vs. physical Jews, it is the latter he has in mind (he is *not* talking about Gentiles here!). The authentic Jew is one who is circumcised within, in the heart, but they still *must be physically Jewish, not Gentile!*

Those who died in the wilderness under God's judgment were circumcised *outwardly*, but not *inwardly*. They were, however, still Jewish by *ethnicity*. While circumcision was an outward sign of the covenant with God, it means nothing without the inward circumcision of the heart which is even more important to God.

So these circumcised, yet unfaithful, Jews fell in the wilderness. At the end of the book of Numbers, every last individual from that previous generation who had rebelled died in the desert. God was again ready to see if the nation of Israel was willing to take Him at His Word. This they did, at least partway. They went into the land and *began* possessing it, this time under Joshua's leadership.

This narrative is only one example of many showing that God deals with Israel as a nation, as one unit. The nation often suffered as a whole due to the actions of one. Conversely, the entire nation is often blessed due to the leadership of one (Moses) and God's work on his behalf. What *one* suffers, they all suffer, until either God's forgiveness is provided, or His judgment, or both. Then Israel starts over with God once again, having come back into fellowship with Him.

This is the way it was for Israel and this is the way it *is* with Israel, in a stage of unbelief. Ezekiel prophesied about this current situation: that they would return to the land in unbelief (Ezekiel 20:30-38). This is exactly the situation since 1948.

The Regathering of Jews to Israel: Prophecy or Wannabe?
If the regathering of Jews back to Israel is a fulfillment of what is written in Ezekiel 20 as well as other places in Scripture, it is obviously God who is bringing this about. If that is the case, then the Anti-Zionist is fighting God, and this is most assuredly a losing battle.

The Anti-Zionist crowd needs to repent, and they need to do it immediately, or they will suffer the consequences of having worked *against* God, *against* His plan and *against* His nation. It is that simple. With respect to the nature of God's covenantal promises made to Abraham, it is with those promises that the entire saga of Israel's history begins, and it is there also that the *unconditional* nature of the Abrahamic Covenant is seen.

Ezekiel 20:30-38

"As I live, declares the Lord GOD, surely with a mighty hand and an outstretched arm and with wrath poured out I will be king over you. I will bring you out from the peoples and gather you out of the countries where you are scattered, with a mighty hand and an outstretched arm, and with wrath poured out. And I will bring you into the wilderness of the peoples, and there I will enter into judgment with you face to face. As I entered into judgment with your fathers in the wilderness of the land of Egypt, so I will enter into judgment with you, declares the Lord GOD. I will make you pass under the rod, and I will bring you into the bond of the covenant. I will purge out the rebels from among you, and those who transgress against me. I will bring them out of the land where they sojourn, but they shall not enter the land of Israel. Then you will know that I am the LORD."

This particular passage is spoken *by* the Lord, *to* Israel, *through* the prophet Ezekiel. We are blessed to have it recorded for us so that *we* know what God is going to do. In spite of this written record, many continue to misunderstand and misinterpret what God is saying with respect to Israel.

In short, God is telling Israel that He *will* be their King, whether they like it or not, and He *will* make sure that they *like* it when He has finished with them. Anyone among the Israelites who does not like it will be purged out. This is not a pleasant picture because we see that the Lord is basically saying the following things to His wayward wife:

- He will bend their will to His and be King over Israel
- He will gather them from where they have been scattered

- Again He mentions that wrath will be poured out on Israel
- He will take them aside and deal with them face to face
- He reminds Israel about the judgment He entered into with their forefathers in the wilderness
- He will force Israel to pass under the rod[8]
- God will enforce His covenant with Israel
- He will eradicate any rebellious Jew among the nation
- The rebels will not be allowed into the Land of Israel
- Because of all this, Israel will know beyond doubt that God is the LORD

Valley of Dry Bones

We have already dealt with this section of Scripture, but a few more notes are important. We know this section begins with a grim picture of dry, dead bones in the valley, which are completely lifeless. In verse four of chapter thirty-seven of Ezekiel, the Lord tells Ezekiel to prophesy over the dead bones. Ezekiel does so and witnesses *"a sound, and behold, a rattling, and the bones came together, bone to its bone. And I looked, and behold, there were sinews on them, and flesh had come upon them, and skin had covered them. But there was no breath in them"* (Ezekiel 37:7b-8).

Ezekiel is told that he should prophesy again. He does so and *"the breath came into them, and they lived and stood on their feet, an exceedingly great army"* (Ezekiel 37:10).

In the final phase of this event, we read: *"Then he said to me, 'Son of man, these bones are the whole house of Israel. Behold, they say, "Our bones are dried up, and our hope is lost; we are indeed cut off." Therefore prophesy, and say to them, Thus says the Lord GOD: Behold, I*

---

[8] "Passing under the rod" is a figure of speech which is indicative of those times when kings would conquer a nation. They would force the leaders, rulers and diplomats of that conquered nation to literally bend over and pass under a rod that was held about waist high. This was symbolically saying that they were bowing to their new ruler.

will open your graves and raise you from your graves, O my people. And I will bring you into the land of Israel. And you shall know that I am the LORD, when I open your graves, and raise you from your graves, O my people. And I will put my Spirit within you, and you shall live, and I will place you in your own land. Then you shall know that I am the LORD; I have spoken, and I will do it, declares the LORD" (Ezekiel 37:11-14).

Here clearly what was once *dead* has been given *life*, over a three-stage process. It did not all occur at once. In spite of how people try to mitigate the importance of this passage (or wrongly attempt to apply this to the Church), God Himself has stated in the text that the bones *"are the whole house of Israel."* This is in keeping with the way God has always dealt with Israel, the nation. He has done so by seeing all of Israel as one unit. Remember, though; when Israel is eventually completely restored, we are at that point talking about the *Remnant* for that period of time which receives Christ just as you and I received Christ for salvation. This will occur during the Tribulation period.

Thomas Ice comments on these events in Ezekiel as related to the house of Israel: *"Ezekiel 20:33-38 speaks of a regathering, which must take place before the tribulation. The passage speaks of bringing the nation of Israel back 'from the peoples and gather you from the lands where you are scattered, with a mighty hand and with an outstretched arm and with wrath poured out' (Ezek. 20:34). 'With wrath poured out' is a descriptive reference to the tribulation. Thus, in order for this to occur in history, Israel must be back in the land before the tribulation. This passage clearly says that it is the Lord who is bringing them back. The current nation of Israel is in the process of fulfilling this passage.*

"In a similar vein, two chapters later, Ezekiel receives another revelation about a future regathering of national Israel (Ezek. 22:17-22). This time, the Lord is 'going to gather you into the midst of Jerusalem' (Ezek. 22:19). Like the metallurgist, the Lord will use the fire of the tribulation to purge out the unfaithful. The Lord is going to

'gather you [Israel] and blow on you with the fire of My wrath, and you will be melted in the midst of it' (Ezek. 22:21). Once again, 'My wrath' depicts the time of the tribulation. It also follows here that the nation must be regathered before that event can take place. The outcome of this event will be that the nation 'will know that I, the Lord, have poured out My wrath on you' (Ezek. 22:22). For this to occur, there must be a regathering by the Lord of Israel to the land, just like we see happening with the modern state of Israel. God is at work through the current state of Israel.

"Surely, anyone who claims to believe in a national future for Israel would have to say that the valley of dry bones prophecy in some way, shape, or form relates to modern Israel (Ezek.37:1-14). The prophet describes a future process through which the nation of Israel will come to be reconstituted and (when the process is complete) enter a faithful spiritual relationship with the Lord. This multi stage process must surely include the current nation of Israel, in unbelief, that is being prepared to go through a time that will lead to her conversion to Jesus as their Messiah. This is said by Ezekiel to be a work of the Lord (Ezek. 37:14).Thus, the modern state of Israel is a work of God and biblically significant."[9]

Various Interpretations

Generally, the Covenant or Replacement Theologian has this to say about the interpretation related to the Valley of Dry Bones in Ezekiel: "Ezekiel's vision probably does not describe a real valley of dry bones, nor does it probably correspond to any real valley with which Ezekiel or his contemporaries were familiar. The ancient Hebrew practice was not to leave dead bodies exposed to the elements, but rather to bury them. There is also no historical record of such a valley. Finally, many of the things that Ezekiel saw in his other visions were not depictions of actual things in the world.

---

[9] http://www.pre-trib.org/article-view.php?id=40

*"The text itself does not seem to indicate that Ezekiel was appalled by this vision, but then again, it does not relate every important feature of his reception of the vision. Rather, it relates primarily those details that are important to its interpretation. Certainly, reading the vivid description of the valley and the regeneration of the bodies is somewhat odd, perhaps even appalling, in some sense. Even so, the **ultimate point of the passage is not just to horrify us with gruesome details, but to give us hope in the new life that God brings to these dead bones.**"*[10] (emphasis added)

Allegorizing Away the Truth
As seen, the Covenant/Replacement Theologian simply allegorizes the Scripture into a different meaning, in which that meaning is truncated into a very pedestrian generalization. In the last portion that I have bolded, notice that the person who penned that response simply believes that all people who are lost, but eventually become Christians, are represented by the dead bones, and God brings life to those who become His through faith in Christ. This is in spite of the fact that the text specifically states that God tells Ezekiel that the bones *represent the whole house of Israel*. This is simply changing God's Words to mean something that they did not originally mean. This is done by removing the text from its context.

In order for the Covenant/Replacement Theologian to acknowledge that the bones represent the whole house of Israel *today*, it would have to be admitted that this event witnessed by Ezekiel is yet to occur with Israel. History shows that there has never been a time when God has ever resurrected the nation of Israel from a completely dead state before 1948, when Israel became a sovereign nation once again. This is then the obvious beginning of the fulfillment of this passage in Ezekiel.

---

[10] http://thirdmill.org/answers/answer.asp/file/99828.qna/category/ot/page/questions/site/iiim

The theologian who stands opposed to a literal interpretation of Scripture is forced to allegorize the message so that it fits the presuppositions brought to bear on Scripture. It is believed that God fully, finally and completely rejected Israel when the nation's leaders rejected the Messiah. Because this belief by Anti-Zionists is firm, it is natural for them to conclude that Israel's future contains nothing. As far as God is concerned, He is only dealing with the Church. He has no more dealings with the nation of Israel.

In that sense, then, the fact of Israel's statehood has become a major thorn in the flesh to those who set themselves *against* Israel. Their view requires them to view her 1948 statehood as either an accident of nature or possibly just one more proof of the stubbornness of Jewish people in general. Certainly, it is not believed that God was involved in the 1948 statehood, nor do they believe He is in any way involved with Israel today. It goes without saying that He will have no involvement with them as a nation in the future either, no matter how the Jews try to find a place for themselves in the Middle East.

This is why those who believe the Church replaced Israel become annoyed and even angered at what is happening in the Middle East today. They see Israel's presence there as due to their rebellious nature. Since Israel is in continued rebellion against God, then all "acts of aggression" by Israel simply heap sin upon sin.

Anger Over God's Plans for Israel
Since these theologians interpret Scripture as they do, God seems to have given them over to blindness regarding His plans for Israel. Due to their blindness, they easily become offended and angered when discussing Israel. They have not merely rejected Israel or the Jewish people, but have rejected *God's purposes for* Israel. *That* is a very serious matter, to say the least.

This seems to be true with anyone who claims to be a Christian yet believes and espouses viewpoints which are inconsistent with the

Word of God. Unmasked anger directed toward those who disagree with them could very well be a telltale sign of their Scriptural error.

Another interpretive effort of a group that proclaims they stand for "Salvation of America and the Nation of Israel" has this to say about the Valley of the Dry Bones: *"This story of the dry bones is often mistaken for the re-gathering of Israel that has taken place in our time. The common belief among many is that at the time Israel was established as a nation in 1948 that the fulfillment of the prophecy about the valley of dry bones had come to pass. Many theologians today are agreeing with this belief, that the fulfillment of these scriptures has been taking place since 1948. Most of the people that believe this...likely have good intentions, [though have little to no understanding of biblical prophecies concerning Israel.] Israel will not be allowed to fully enjoy the Land as an eternal possession until Israel has accepted Jesus Christ as their savior. God himself will not allow it. And this is what the valley of dry bones is all about. It tells of the spiritual rebirth of Israel. The valley of dry bones is a symbolic representation of Israel's spiritual state with God. [It is very much like that of any person who is not born again. Before the new birth, the individual is spiritually dead, in trespasses and sins.] In the vision of the valley of dry bones, we are told that the bones are very dry (verse 2). This reinforces just how spiritually dead Israel is in this prophecy."*[11]

Regathered in Unbelief by God's Own Hand

In studying the above quote, it seems clear that a lack of understanding with respect to the meaning of the vision exists. The individual first states that the Ezekiel passage was *not* fulfilled in 1948, then states that Israel will not possess the land until they receive Jesus Christ as Savior. He doesn't realize that the resurrection of the dry bones occurs in *stages*, starting with a regathering in *unbelief*.

---

[11] http://www.americaisraelprophecy.com/drybones.html

If he and others would look closely at the passage, the entire content deals with a *process* over a period time. As we have already indicated, there is a three-part restoration of Israel by God. In the end, the Remnant of Israel *will* know Christ as Messiah, Savior and Lord *before* they go in to possess the land after the Great Tribulation. It will be on this basis that they will be *allowed* to enter the land.

The other difficulty with the above interpretation lies in the fact that the passage in Ezekiel is only *one* such passage discussing the regathering of Israel. There are many others, including passages from Jeremiah and Isaiah, as just two examples. The individual quoted above does not realize that, from God's own Words, we know that He will be regathering Israel in *wrath* with an *outstretched arm*. The implication here is that Israel will be regathered, but they will *not* be saved at that time. Their regathering will allow God to literally deal with their rebellious nature. This will be dealt with *once and for all* during the Great Tribulation, also known as the *time of Jacob's trouble*, or the *time of distress for Jacob* (Jeremiah 30:7).

The Jewish people will return to the Land, thinking *they* are the ones who have decided to return, when in point of fact, it is God who has caused them to return. The major reason for the Great Tribulation is to *purify* Israel by filtering out the rebels (cf. Ezekiel 20), with the Remnant *remaining* after the rebels have been purged from Israel.

It is this Remnant which Paul is referring to in Romans 11:26, which will be saved and will take possession of the Land at the end of the Great Tribulation. The Remnant will fulfill what Christ prophesied in Matthew 23:39 when He specifically stated (to Israel): "*I tell you, you will not see me again, until you say, 'Blessed is he who comes in the name of the Lord.'*" Take a look at that chapter. Everything Christ is saying is directed *to* Israel and Israel's religious leaders. The Church is not there. She is not there because the Church does *not* need to be purified, because as Paul clearly explains, this has already occurred (Ephesians 1:3;18-19;2:5-6).

Here is the passage from Ezekiel:

"*Ezekiel 37: 12: Therefore prophesy and say unto them, Thus saith the Lord GOD; Behold, O my people, I will open your graves, and cause you to come up out of your graves, and bring you into the land of Israel. 13: And ye shall know that I am the LORD, when I have opened your graves, O my people, and brought you up out of your graves, 14: And shall **put my spirit in you, and ye shall live**, and **I shall place you in your own land**: then shall ye know that I the LORD have spoken it, and performed it, saith the LORD.*"[12]

In spite of the above, our friend states this: "*You must realize that this verse is the bottom line for the teaching on the valley of dry bones. It concludes by revealing the mystery of this vision. God was telling Ezekiel that there was a day coming that God would put his spirit in the* **hearts of the people of Israel and that they would come alive**. *This is exactly what he has done with* **every born again believer from the time of the Disciples until today**. *His spirit in us is what makes us alive unto God. We are born again.*

"*There are three things that is revealed to us in these scriptures:*

1. *That Israel will be born again.*
2. *This will happen before Israel is resurrected.*
3. *After they are born again and resurrected from the dead,* **God takes them back to the land of Israel.**"[13] (emphasis added)

Instead of understanding the literal meaning of the text, our friend allegorizes the text and superimposes it on top of the Church. He agrees that God is speaking to Israel and he agrees that the references to Israel are clear. Yet, all of a sudden, he jumps from Israel to the Church, and he does this – as many do – based on a

---

[12] http://www.americaisraelprophecy.com/drybones.html
[13] http://www.americaisraelprophecy.com/drybones.html

faulty understanding of Romans 9-11. In that section of Scripture, Paul teaches the difference between a spiritual Jew and one who is merely a physical Jew. In both cases, the individuals are *Jewish*, not *Gentile*!

So this person, as well as many others, *assumes* that the references directed to Israel *now* refer to the Church. It is obvious that God *will* put His Spirit within all people who come to know Him as Savior and Lord. Salvation is exactly the same for Jewish people as well as Gentiles. However, what this individual is doing is making the mistake of thinking that God's salvation for *all* is the same as His *will* for all, which is not the case.

God still has a mighty work to perform in Israel. He will do this for the sake of His Name, not for the sake of Israel. The Old Testament is filled with promises made directly *to* the nation of Israel. Many of those promises have not been fulfilled and will *not* be fulfilled in the Church. Because God wants to literally *clear* His Name, He will bring His promises to Israel to fruition.

Toward the end of the Great Tribulation, when God's predetermined Jewish Remnant finally realizes their lost condition, they will *earnestly* pray and plead for the return of the Messiah (Matthew 23:39). In response, Christ will physically return to *be* their Messiah. The change that will take place within them is exactly what took place within the one thief who hung next to Jesus as the life blood ebbed from both of them.

The Example of the Thief on the Cross

In Luke 23, we read the short narrative of the thief on the cross. One moment, he was ridiculing, reviling and blaspheming the Lord, and the next, his eyes were open to the truth of Christ's identity. With this new understanding, he turned to Christ in repentance and simplicity, asking only that he be "remembered" when Christ came into His kingdom. He had obviously gotten to the point of realizing that Christ was, in fact, *a King!* This knowledge underscored his need to repent, and prompted him to plead before this King for the smallest of requests, that he merely be *remembered*.

Christ turned to him, stating just as simply, *"I tell you the truth, today you will be with me in paradise"* (Luke 23:43). What caused such a drastic change within the heart of the thief? It was the removal of his blinders by the Holy Spirit, which allowed the Truth to penetrate to his soul.

Paul says, in effect, that Israel has been blinded for the sake of the Gentiles: *"Rather through [Israel's] trespass [of rebellion leading to their current blindness] salvation has come to the Gentiles, so as to make Israel jealous. Now if their trespass means riches for the world, and if their failure means riches for the Gentiles, how much more will their full inclusion mean!"* (Romans 11:11b-12)

As the thief hung dying next to Christ, he was originally blind to Christ's true nature. However, at one point, his heart was enlightened to that truth. There was absolutely *nothing* that this thief could have done to open his own eyes. For reasons known only to God, He chose to bless this man with the knowledge of the Holy and opened his eyes. Once he saw the truth, it became *his* responsibility to acknowledge and receive that truth. This he did, which led to the reward of eternal life.

The Blindness of Today's Jew

As Paul stated, the Jews have been *temporarily* blinded in order for God to extend salvation to the Gentiles *without* having to go through the nation of Israel first. This is how things were done in the Old Testament (Exodus 13:3) concerning people outside the nation of Israel. Anyone who wanted to worship Israel's God had to become part of that nation, converting *to* Judaism *from* paganism.

Because God hardened their hearts *after* their rejection of Jesus, He was then able to reach out directly to Gentiles, bypassing the religious leaders and the nation of Israel completely. The Gentiles would now benefit from Israel's blindness because God now reaches out to the Gentile *directly*. It is Israel's blindness which literally *forwarded to the Gentiles* the saving grace of Christ through His atonement.

As noted in our Romans 11 quote, Paul speaks of the fact that he wants as many Gentiles as possible to become saved, not only for their sake, but also in order to make the Jewish people jealous – jealous enough to return to God through Jesus Christ!

Anti-Zionists Say: Rejection By God is Final
Anti-Zionists teach that once the leaders of Israel rejected Christ, God's love for Israel waned, growing permanently cold. God forever and finally rejected Israel as a nation. We are also told by these same individuals that there is *no chance* of God ever *forgiving* or reestablishing ties with the nation of Israel directly. The most that the Jewish people can expect today is individual salvation. The nation of Israel is gone, forever blended into and replaced by the Church, which has taken over Israel's favored position and promises.

It is through our union with Christ that Christians (from both Jew and Gentile people groups) are united in Christ as *one* entity. But it is also *because* of this union with Christ that there is no further need for the nation of Israel. Israel as a nation was merely a shadow of the reality now found in Christ.

Since many individuals see Christian Zionism as an affront to God's grace and love, then it is viewed as evil, needing to be stamped out. Nevertheless, this provides no excusable reason for the vitriol and vehemence with which these individuals continually and verbally assault Christian Zionism. The Christian Zionist is also seen as the modern day Pharisee by many within Anti-Zionism. An article written by Charles E. Carlson titled *Kulchur Klash 2002: Part 1* states the following:

"Many of these self-professed Christian leaders are the Pharisees of today, achieving fame and influence by pleasing the secular Zionist media powers.

"Pharisees were once exclusively Judean, 'Jews' in the vernacular of our day. Many contend that Israeli Patriots assert more control over America's political parties, news media and the banking system than is healthy for a Christian society. This should be obvious to anyone who will look at the media; then read the Bible references to Pharisaism. But it is largely from within that the vitality of Christianity is being diluted, not from outside. The control of media may be a 'Jewish' problem, but the perversion of Christianity is not. Many professing Christians at all levels of leadership have abandoned their Bible given responsibility in exchange for the footnotes written by men. These are the Pharisees of today."

In the above quote, Carlson condemns those said to have abandoned their Bible, preferring instead the explanatory notes written by men. He is referring to the study notes written by people like Scofield and those who have followed suit. Note how Carlson barely masks his rancor, which seem to ooze from the very words themselves. Note also how he places quotes around the word *Jews* and *Jewish*, as if merely writing the words fills him with disdain.

Since Carlson equates Christian Zionists with the Pharisees, this removes all vestiges of humanity from the *Christian* Zionist. In so doing, all verbal attacks become the accepted way of dealing with Christian Zionism and its adherents. Taking their cue from Christ Himself, who continually upbraided the religious leaders of His day (mainly Pharisees), the Pharisee *should* be attacked. Who does not think of the Pharisee as someone to resolutely *dislike*?

Christ had nothing good thing to say about the Pharisees, did He? For that matter, He said nothing good about the Sadducees or the Scribes either. He went head to head with these groups time after time, repeatedly calling their bluff. He continued His denouncement of them until it was His scheduled time to go to the cross, and then gave Himself to that aspect of the Father's will. While the Pharisees planned to kill Christ many times, they were thwarted by one thing or another because it was not His time.

The Pharisees are seen as standing resolutely against Christ, literally foaming at the mouth in rage, with all of their hypocritical *legalisms* firmly intact. They exhibited no love for anyone, except of course themselves. Their constant twisting of Scripture kept them from receiving salvation and kept others from receiving it as well. They did everything they could to build themselves up, believing in their own self-importance. Then Christ came along, and with scathing verbal agility and accuracy, pronounced judgment on them time and time again.

It needs to be understood that because of their view of Christian Zionism, Anti-Zionists feel justified in delivering their vitriolic attacks toward those who support Israel. It is what Christ did with the Pharisees, is it not? The Christian Zionist deserves the same treatment, says the Anti-Zionist.

The Wife of Jehovah and the Bride of Christ
Getting back to our discussion about the Wife of Jehovah and the Bride of Christ, it should be clear that the Bible is quite obviously referring to *two* distinct groups of people: 1) Israel, the wife of Jehovah, and 2) the Church, the Bride of Christ. The situation in the Old Testament regarding Israel is one in which Jehovah is clearly *already* married to her. There are many occasions in which God says He will give a writ of divorce, proving that the marriage was already in place. As mentioned, the book of Hosea highlights the fact that God *did* divorce Israel. Yet, He did not leave her in that position. He

was always wooing her back to Him (cf. Hosea 2:16, 19-20; Isaiah 54:5-8, etc.). It is unthinkable to believe that God would permanently divorce the very people He had created as special and peculiar people to Himself! Yet this is what the Anti-Zionist expects us to believe.

Regarding the Church, it is nowhere stated that the Church is *currently* married to Jesus. The fact of a marriage is yet future. The marriage feast, the ceremony, all of it will occur in a future time after Christ's Bride has been received to Him. It is completely incorrect to interchange these two phrases – *the wife of Jehovah* and *the Bride of Christ* – as *if* they refer to the same set of people, because they do *not*.

The Wife of Jehovah has *always* been associated with Jehovah and the Bride of Christ has *always* been connected to Jesus. Since Jehovah and Christ are two different Persons within the Godhead, it is not only incorrect to mix them, but it is unbiblical to do so.

Supporting Israel
At its root, Christian Zionism takes the position of supporting Israel because it is God's chosen nation. In the opinion of the Christian Zionist, Israel has *not* ceased to be the chosen nation. They are merely set aside temporarily by God until the fullness of the Gentiles comes in, as Paul noted in Romans 9-11.

Beyond this, Anti-Zionists do not see that Christian Zionists are ultimately supporting God and His purposes. These purposes include the Land that is currently being fought over in the Middle East. Throughout the Bible, the Land is described as *His* Land. Jerusalem is described as *His* city. Israel is described as *His* nation.

One particular website says this about Christian Zionism: *"Christian Zionism seeks to declare the truth of God's word that bequeaths to the people of Israel the Land of Canaan as an everlasting possession. This promise was made by God to Abraham some four thousand years ago*

*(Genesis 13:14-18). Moreover, the promise was reiterated time and time again and stressed that loss of domicile, because of rebellion and disobedience, **would not mean loss of possession** (Deuteronomy 30:1-6). The God who exiled the Jewish People on two occasions -586 B.C. and 70 A.D.- has always promised to bring them back and restore their fortunes (Jeremiah 31:10 and Isaiah 11:11). All this because of His promise to Abraham.*[14] (emphasis added)

At its core, that is what Christian Zionism believes. The same website continues with: "*From time to time Christian Zionists have been upbraided for leaning too heavily upon the Old Testament for verification of their stand and belief. However, the biblical foundation of Christian Zionism is also found in the New Testament.*[15] This is the clear teaching of Scripture regarding the future scattering of the Jewish people (cf. Luke 21).

Jesus also clearly stated the *regathering* of Israel would occur way into the future, and He described the events surrounding that regathering. It becomes obvious after a careful reading of specific portions of Scripture that God has *not* fully and finally rejected the nation of Israel. To *not* understand this will give rise to erroneous theology. God's plan *does* include regathering *His* people back to *His* land.

---

[14] http://christianactionforisrael.org/4thcongress2.html
[15] Ibid

11

The Spiritual Jew

The line of demarcation between the Church and Israel has become extremely blurred by those who see no unique plan in God's purposes for the future state of Israel. Since it is too often stated that Israel has actually been replaced by the Church, it is commonplace in today's church-going society to hear Christians refer to themselves as "spiritual Jews" or "real Jews," though they are *Gentile* Christians. These Christians are unfortunately misunderstanding Paul's simple and clear teachings in Romans where he discusses what it means to be a true Jew.

In the context of those passages, Paul is not referring *to* Gentiles. He is dealing specifically with Jewish individuals at that point in Romans. He is making a distinction between a true Jew and a false Jew, but *both* are Jews. This is important to grasp because it sets the stage for what he eventually says about the nation of Israel later in Romans.

Paul's Words and Teachings
In looking at the book of Romans, then, we must understand that Paul begins in chapter one by explaining that no one is free from guilt and all are under judgment: the Jew, the Gentile, the pagan etc. Paul then discusses each ethnicity individually so that he cannot be misunderstood.

The clear difference between Christian Zionism and those diametrically opposed to it stems from how one understands Paul's statements in Romans chapters nine through eleven. We all read the same words that Paul wrote, yet we do not all come away with the same meaning.

One author makes a number of statements about the real identity of the seed of Abraham and what constitutes a real Jew. It will be helpful to look at how this individual interprets Paul's words, and we can then compare that to Scripture to determine if they are correct or not.

Who is the True Jew?
"Paul's definition of who is an heir of Abraham and who is not, [is] revealed primarily in the third and fourth chapters of Galatians and the ninth through eleventh chapters of Romans."[16] This same individual – Theodore Winston Pike – continues by first looking at Romans chapter nine. *"St. Paul drops a theological bombshell. He states that not everyone who is born of Jewish parents and educated in*

---

[16] Theodore Winston Pike, *Israel Our Duty...Our Dilemma* (Big Sky Press 2003), 8

the synagogue is a Jew. 'For they are not all Israel which are Israel: Neither, because they are the seed of Abraham, are they all children: but, In Isaac shall thy seed be called. That is, they which are the children of the flesh, these are not the children of God: but the children of the promise are counted for the seed' (Romans 9:6-8)."[17]

Immediately after this statement, Pike announces "*Good orthodox Jews of pure descent are 'not the seed of Abraham'? Can the earth bear such words? Did not Paul realize that the Christian church today stands trembling before the Jew because it believes him to be the 'seed of Abraham,' inheritor of his ancient patriarchal privileges, and that the nation of Israel lays claim to Palestine because such was promised to the 'seed of Abraham'?*"[18]

Unfortunately, Pike has already got it terribly wrong. Notice that he is not only convinced that he has it *correct*, but his foray into sarcasm underscores that point. Pike maintains that "*Good orthodox Jews of pure descent are 'not the seed of Abraham,'*" which is presented as a sweeping generalization. What he seems to mean is that **no** Jewish person is really the true seed of Abraham. This is a complete misunderstanding of Paul's words. This type of mistake is extremely easy to make if the *context* of the text is ignored. Paul is, in fact, making no such comment. He is not *eliminating* Jewish individuals at all.

If we consider the biblical text of Romans closely, Paul is actually saying that just because someone *comes from Abraham's seed*, it does not make them a true, *spiritual* Jew any more than being part of Israel in the Old Testament made someone part of the Remnant. Put another way, Paul affirms that it is only those Jewish people who are "born again" whom he calls "spiritual Jews" from Abraham's seed.

---

[17] Ibid, 8
[18] Theodore Winston Pike, *Israel Our Duty...Our Dilemma* (Big Sky Press 2003), 9

These individuals *believe* God and are saved because of it, just as Abraham was and just as Gentiles are saved.

However, let us continue with our friend Pike, whom we have quoted above, to see where he goes with this line of thinking. He asks, who makes up the actual Remnant? He says, *"Paul tells us the true 'seed' of Abraham constitutes a pure remnant in every age, which has been chosen by God for salvation."*[19]

So far, so good. This is exactly what Paul is saying. Just because someone is a Jew, it does not mean that they are part of the Remnant. Just so that we are clear, though, one must ask: exactly *where* did God keep that Remnant? It was always hidden *within* the nation of Israel, *never* outside of Israel, within other nations.

Our friend Pike continues, *"Hebrew Christians constituted the descendants of a 'remnant' within Israel, which had always existed in its center, despite the apostasy surrounding."*[20] This is good, and Pike continues to be right on track here.

Pike then states, *"Paul continues to equate the New Testament church with this remnant, repeating God's answer to Elijah after his victory over the prophets of Baal on Mt. Carmel...in Romans 11:7, St. Paul describes this Christian* **Remnant as those who had really grasped the meaning of Israel.** *Israel of the flesh did not comprehend their Messiah – only Israel of the spirit, for the rest were blinded."*[21] (emphasis added)

Whoops!! Our friend was doing *so well*, until he made this huge jump by going completely *away* from Israel to the Church. Yet, it is clear from the earlier text in Romans chapter nine, that Paul only had *Jewish individuals* in mind, *not* Gentiles. In fact, though he points out

---

[19] Ibid, 9
[20] Theodore Winston Pike, *Israel Our Duty...Our Dilemma* (Big Sky Press 2003), 10
[21] Ibid, 10

in chapter nine of Romans that salvation is for *both* the Jew and the Gentiles, Paul goes right back to the Israeli remnant by quoting Isaiah: *"Though the number of the sons of Israel be as the sand of the sea, only a remnant of them will be saved"* (Romans 9:27).

I have heard it said that the reference to Israel "as the sand of the sea" could not possibly be simply referring *only* to Jewish individuals. Therefore, Isaiah must have included Christian Gentiles too. This is going way beyond the meaning of the text, though. It is clear from the OT alone that the Israelites, upon exiting Egypt, could have had numbers totaling six hundred three thousand five hundred fifty (cf. Numbers 1:46). If that was the original number of people *leaving* Egypt at the beginning of their travels, it should not be difficult to believe that their numbers would grow so large that they would become like the sand of the sea.

However, it *is* also possible that God *was* referencing the total number of people who would become heirs to *salvation* that came from Abraham's seed, Jesus Christ. This is certainly possible. Even this, though, does not negate the other promises that God made to Abraham. In fact, if this is what God meant, then it confirms that the other promises made to Abraham were just as valid.

In the quote above, Pike makes the grand mistake of taking Paul's words like *"my brethren," "my kinsman,"* or *"my people"* to mean *Gentiles*, when in point of fact, the *entire context* is referencing Jewish individuals. This makes sense given that Paul himself, while a Christian, is *still* Jewish. Being Jewish reflects a person's *ethnicity*. This does not change even after becoming a believer. In fact, while on earth, *no person's* ethnicity or gender changes after becoming a Christian. Men don't stop being men, nor do women stop being women.

Alan Nairne goes so far as to say that *"We must conclude from these Scriptures that the olive tree of Romans chapter eleven is nothing less than the totality of the promises to Abraham."*[22] But this conclusion is hardly logical, given the fact that Paul has been comparing *unregenerate* Jewish people with *regenerate* Jewish people. The *only* promise that is extended to everyone regardless of ethnicity, nationality, or gender is that of *salvation* through the Redeemer, Jesus Christ.

In chapter eleven of Romans, Paul is clearly referring to Jews *from* Israel. He also refers to how Elijah felt as if he was the *only* person who stood for God, yet it turned out not to be the case. Paul says, *"I ask, then, has God rejected his people? By no means! For I myself am an Israelite, a descendant of Abraham, a member of the tribe of Benjamin. God has not rejected his people whom he foreknew. Do you not know what the Scripture says of Elijah, how he appeals to God against Israel? 'Lord, they have killed your prophets, they have demolished your altars, and I alone am left, and they seek my life.' But what is God's reply to him? 'I have kept for myself seven thousand men who have not bowed the knee to Baal.' So too at the present time there is a remnant, chosen by grace. But if it is by grace, it is no longer on the basis of works; otherwise grace would no longer be grace"* (Romans 11:1-6).

Nairne, Pike and others seem unable to recognize the fact that this Remnant that God spoke of with Elijah came *directly from* within Israel. Pike believes that Paul is referring to some "Christian" Remnant (whatever that is), referencing, *"In Romans 11:7, St. Paul describes this Christian remnant as those who had really grasped the meaning of Israel. Israel of the flesh did not comprehend their Messiah – only Israel of the spirit, for the rest were blinded."* In spite of what Pike believes, this is an obvious reference to the state of Israel as a nation and the Remnant *within* Israel.

---

[22] http://www.apocalipsis.org/Israel.htm

Dr. Arnold G. Fruchtenbaum comments on this situation for us. He states, *"The point of verses 1-10 then, is that while Israel as a nation has failed to attain righteousness, this rejection of the Messiahship of Jesus is not a total rejection; there are Jewish people who do believe. These Jewish believers have attained the righteousness of God. At the present time, there are Jewish believers that are the Remnant according to the election of grace. So instead of using the existence of a minority of believers as evidence that God has cast off His people, in reality, it is evidence that He has not."*[23]

So it should be clear that the Remnant is *not* made up of Jewish people and Gentile people. The Remnant includes those Jewish people from the nation of Israel. If we understand Paul to be stating this, then the entire Olive Tree scenario becomes plainly clear.

Paul's point, according to Dr. Fruchtenbaum (and one in which this author is in agreement), is that God has vouchsafed His Remnant by placing it *alongside* the Church (during this current period of history), but the entirety of the Church is *not* the Remnant. Do you see the difference? In actuality, the Church is *attached* to the Remnant.

Dr. Fruchtenbaum continues: *"The point Paul makes is that it was God's plan for Israel to reject the Messiahship of Jesus for a while, [so that] the gospel would go out to the Gentiles, during which time they were to provoke Jews to jealousy; until eventually, all Israel is saved. Paul builds upon Isaiah 49:1-13, where Isaiah taught the same thing: that the Messiah would come to Israel, Israel would reject Him, and the Messiah would then, for a while, become the light to the Gentiles; but eventually, Israel [as a nation <u>from</u> the Remnant] will return to Him and be restored."*[24]

---

[23] Arnold Fruchtenbaum, *Footsteps of the Messiah* (San Antonio, Ariel Ministries), 783
[24] Arnold Fruchtenbaum, *Footsteps of the Messiah* (San Antonio, Ariel Ministries), 783

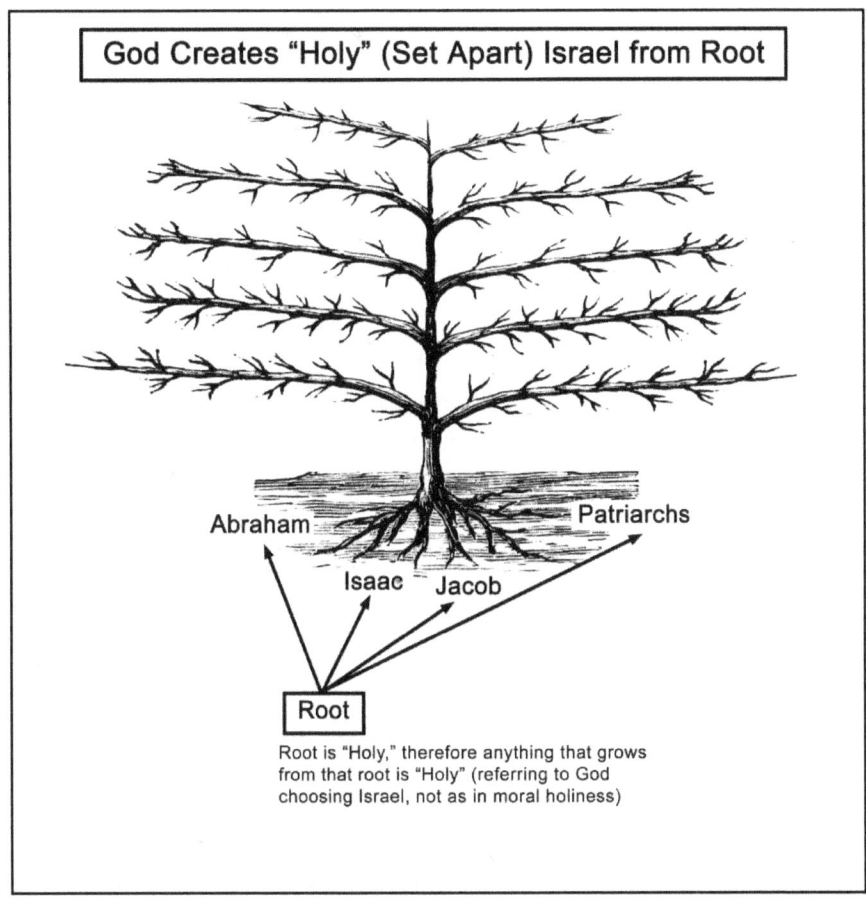

To misinterpret Paul's clear teaching leads directly to the error that the Church has permanently replaced Israel. This belief is arrived at only by *erroneously* interpreting the passages here in Romans and elsewhere, normally through the use of allegory.

A careful reading of the entire book of Romans, with special emphasis on chapters nine through eleven, reveals that this belief about the Church replacing Israel is a completely *false* notion, yet people continue to support it. It is an untenable position arrived at by either ignoring or misconstruing the context. In spite of this, though, Anti-Zionists state that *their* belief is the correct one and the

Christian Zionist suffers from a case of badly misinterpreting Scripture.

So how do we determine which belief is the correct belief? Like anything else, it can only be accomplished through the careful exegesis of God's Word. His Word must be studied in all its fullness, allowing Scripture to interpret Scripture, in order to arrive at the correct conclusion. Sifting through the complexities of Scripture can be difficult because of the many things that need to be considered in order to arrive at the proper conclusion. We have begun to do this, but let's take the time to look even more closely at the Olive Tree and see what God's Word states.

The Olive Tree
Paul continues his argument by using the example of an Olive Tree (cf. Romans 11:11-24). The main point of Paul's teaching regarding the Olive Tree is that it represents what Dr. Fruchtenbaum and other commentators refer to as the place of *blessing*. It does *not* represent an individual's salvation.

Just as some of the natural Jewish branches were pruned off and wild Gentile olive branches grafted in, God can just as easily reverse the situation. This is why Paul is so careful to insist that the Gentiles should not boast in any way at all about the fact that some Jewish branches have been removed to make room for Gentile branches. It is *God* who does the pruning and grafting, and it is *He* who receives the praise and glory. This cannot refer to *salvation*, as it is something that is eternally guaranteed by God, with the Holy Spirit's seal acting as a guarantee.

The Olive Tree's *lump* and *natural branches* also represent Israel (cf. Romans 11:16). The actual *root* of the tree goes all the way back to Abraham, Isaac, Jacob, and the Abrahamic Covenant itself, and the root gave birth to Israel.

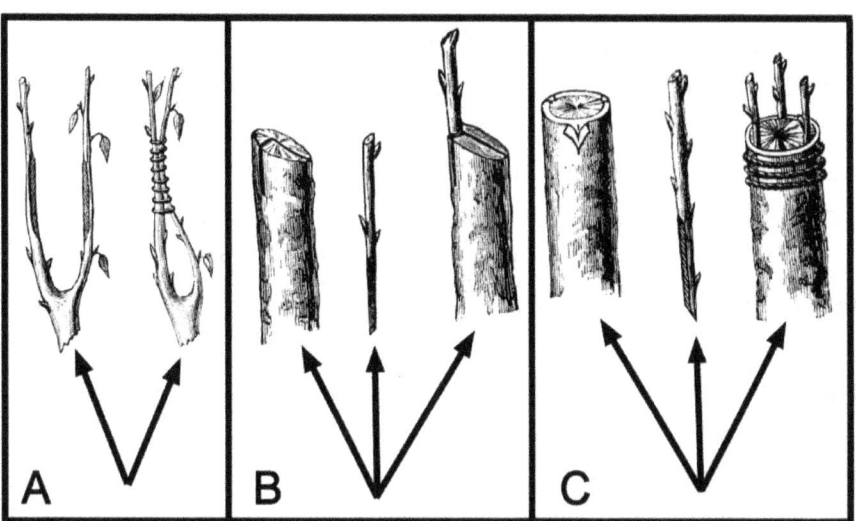

God's Grafting Process for the Church

A B C

There are many ways to graft foreign branches into a tree or vine, as shown by the illustrations A, B, and C. What **never** changes, though, is that the foreign branch that is grafted in, **never** establishes its identity as the original tree. The foreign branch always remains what it was originally created to be, but now, having been grafted into another tree, receives the nutrients and strength that it was unable to obtain by itself.

If not for this tree that the foreign branch was grafted into it would have **died**, but now, because it has been grafted into **another** source that is teaming with life, this foreign branch now thrives. This is the Church. The Church has been grafted into the tree which is not only owned by another (Israel), but we are foreigners to it. In spite of this, though we are blessed to receive from this tree what we would not otherwise be able to obtain without it.

Fruchtenbaum states that *"The Olive Tree in this passage does **not** represent Israel or the Church; it represents the place of spiritual blessing. Israel is the owner of the Olive Tree, but Israel is not the tree itself. The root of this place of blessing is the Abrahamic Covenant. Paul makes the same point here that he made in Ephesians 2:11-16 and*

3:5-6...The Gentiles are not 'takers-over,' but 'partakers of Jewish spiritual blessings.'"[25]

Gentiles Grafted *Into* the Olive Tree

The entire Olive Tree is of *Jewish* origin! Please note that Gentiles (Christians) are grafted *into the Olive Tree*. It is *not* the other way around. The Jews who are believers are *not* being grafted into anything *Gentile*. This is extremely important to understand. In essence, then, Christian Gentiles are now receiving the *blessings* of salvation *because they have been grafted into* the Olive Tree owned by Israel. The Olive Tree always remains Jewish in heritage. Gentiles are privileged to *share* in the *salvific* blessings (of the Abrahamic Covenant) by their connection to the Olive Tree through the grafting process.

Gentiles have *no* claim to the root, the lump, the dough or anything else connected to that tree. Gentile branches are the *wild* branches that essentially do not belong to that tree. God's grace, however, has caused the Gentiles who place their faith in Him to benefit from their association *with* the Olive Tree. This *still* does not mean that Gentile Christians are *spiritual Jews*, any more than an orphaned kitten being nursed by a dog along with her *own* litter of puppies *becomes* a "spiritual" dog.

Toward the end of his book, Pike arrives at an untenable, yet not surprising, conclusion. He without equivocation states that Israel has *no biblical* right to occupy Palestine. This is one of the main tenets of the Replacement Theologian's belief. He arrives there because of his faulty interpretation with respect to Paul's arguments in Romans and Galatians.

Gender and Ethnic Distinctions

Pike uses Galatians as proof that Paul teaches about the type of

---

[25] Arnold G. Fruchtenbaum, *Footsteps of the Messiah* (San Antonio: Ariel Ministries), 784

Israel and the Remnant Within

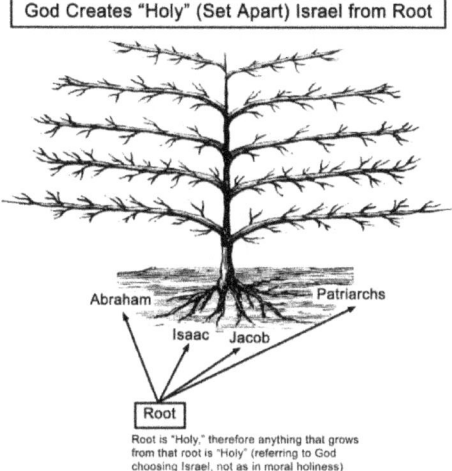

God Creates "Holy" (Set Apart) Israel from Root

Root is "Holy," therefore anything that grows from that root is "Holy" (referring to God choosing Israel, not as in moral holiness)

God has ALWAYS dealt with Israel as ONE nation. Once created, His Remnant was kept INSIDE the nation of Israel. ALL Jews - physical and spiritual - are considered Israelites, but only the **spiritual** Jews are ever part of the TRUE Israel (the Remnant).

Remnant of Israel and the Church

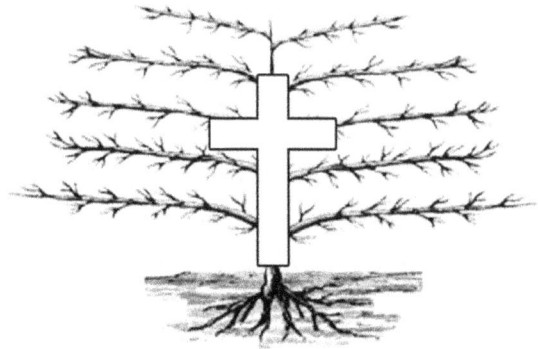

New Testament Period Until Fullness of Gentiles

Once God created the Church (kept secret from the Prophets), He continued with His Remnant, with the Church being established as each new believer is grafted into the same Olive Tree as the Remnant. Once the fullness of Gentiles comes in, God will **Rapture** the Church and once again deal with unregenerate Israel.

person who truly constitutes an *authentic* (or spiritual) Jew. If you are familiar with Galatians, you know that Paul was dealing with the fact that the believers in the churches throughout Galatia were being deceived into thinking that salvation was *not* by grace alone, but was by grace *plus* works. In this case, it was the act of *circumcision*.

Paul goes through the painstaking process of pointing out to the Galatian believers that works of the flesh did *nothing* to save anyone. In fact, he clarifies for them that all who live under the Law are also under a *curse* (cf. Galatians 3:10). This is due to the fact that it is impossible for anyone to uphold every aspect of the Law. Christ – being *fully* God and *fully* Man – was the only One to do it, and of course the blessing of salvation comes to us because of *His* ability to keep the Law, being made perfect in the process.

However, we need to be certain we understand the *context* in which this letter was written by the apostle. Nairne, commenting on Galatians, states, "*The NT makes it quite clear that the nation, land, priesthood, tabernacle, temple, offerings, were, like Eden, and so much else, picture books of the reality that was to come, and a vehicle to ensure that God's Deliverer would be able to come in the 'fulness of time'. What kind of duration was envisaged for the law - and, by implication the nation? 'Until the seed should come to whom the promises were made' (Gal. 3:19).*"[26]

However, we need to ask Nairne *why* he is including all the promises given to Abraham, while Paul is only dealing with *salvation* in Galatians? There is most certainly an *eternal* reality found within the Abrahamic Covenant. It is safe to say that this reality exists within *eternity*, not *time*. The only people who are *currently* experiencing the reality of the priesthood, tabernacle, etc., are those believers who have died and entered into that *eternal* existence in the next life, where Christ is physically seen and experienced.

---

[26] http://www.apocalipsis.org/Israel.htm

By including the nation, land, priesthood, tabernacle, and the rest, as he has done, Nairne *wrongly* assumes that by referring to the Law in Galatians 3, he implies that Paul must be referring to *all aspects* of the Abrahamic Covenant. However, this is not a *realistic* or *accurate* assumption.

The Law given to Israel through Moses was *not* intended to supplant (or even fulfill) all aspects of the Abrahamic Covenant. It was to do two things: 1) *point to the reality that the Law could not bring about salvation,* and 2) *point to the forthcoming eternal salvation which would be available through the Messiah.* So while the Law pointed out the *fact of sin*, it also, by implication, pointed out the *need for a Savior*. Again, though, this is all related to the topic of *salvation* which Paul is covering in Galatians. This is why Paul brings it up in the first place, because of the danger that existed for the Galatian churches. They were being deceived into thinking that going back to the Law was what provided salvation.

Paul states, *"Why then was the law given? It was added because of transgressions, until the arrival of the descendant to whom the promise had been made"* (Galatians 3:19 NET). Regarding the same passage, Nairne states, *"Concerning the covenant at Sinai, we need to understand that, in essence, nothing had changed. Paul tells us (Gal.3:19) that the law was added, or, came alongside, that which was already in existence - i.e. the Abrahamic promises. That is, the Abrahamic covenant 'embraced' the Mosaic covenant. The way of personal salvation, revealed in the Garden of Eden, (Gen.3:21; 4:4) through faith and sacrifice, was still the same for each individual. The 'Law' was given, not to procure salvation, but to provide a format within which godly Hebrews could, as a matter of love to their God, in thankfulness, and in the spirit of the law (see Deut.10:16 & 30:6) live lives that were pleasing to him."*[27]

---

[27] http://www.apocalipsis.org/Israel.htm

While on one hand, Nairne seems to understand that the part of the Abrahamic Covenant that Paul is dealing with in Galatians is the **salvific** part, Nairne unfortunately believes that salvation for Gentiles fulfills or includes *all aspects* of the Abrahamic Covenant. However, this is not true. The atonement of Jesus makes salvation *possible* and makes it so that the remaining aspects of the Abrahamic Covenant *will* occur as well.

Concerning the letter to the Galatians, we know that this letter was written circa A.D. 49. We also know that the book of Acts covers a period of roughly thirty years, so this letter was written about seventeen years into the book of Acts, making the church fairly young at this point. During this time, the majority of the new Church was largely made up of *Jewish* believers, and this is a very important fact which needs to be considered in discerning meaning.

We learn from the book of Acts that as Paul went through the various provinces of Asia and other parts of the known world, he would always go to the Jews *first*. Normally, after he presented the Jewish people with the gospel message in their synagogues, some would hear and receive his message, becoming converted in the process. It was *because of this conversion of Jewish people* that certain Jewish men followed Paul from place to place. They attempted to *undo* what Paul did, and tried to keep him from spreading the message of Christ to *other* Jewish people. When Jewish leaders would eventually reject Paul because of the message he brought, he would *then* normally go to the Gentiles, presenting the same message, where it was usually more eagerly received.

Paul: Persecuted the Church
Paul speaks of persecuting the church in the opening verses of Galatians, chapter one (vv. 13-14) as part of his former life. He speaks of his zeal on behalf of Judaism. He understands *why* there are certain individuals who are literally sneaking in to draw these believers *back* into Judaism (Galatians 1:6-10). Like he *was*, they *are*

misguided. Though they think they are trying to bring wayward brothers back into the fold of Judaism, they are really *perverting* the gospel of Jesus Christ by adding works to the process.

What can we learn from this? I believe the only logical conclusion that we can rightly arrive at is that Paul's primary concern is for *Jewish believers* in the churches in Galatia. Judaizers would not in the least have been concerned about any *Gentiles* who had become Christians. But the *Jews,* who had converted *from* Judaism to Christianity, would have been the people that the Judaizers would have been concerned about.

Before Paul was converted on the road to Damascus, it was not his purpose to go all over the known world chasing down *Gentiles* and hauling them back to Jerusalem. His mission only concerned finding *Jewish individuals* who had *become* Christians. Because of the dispersion of the Christian Jews due to the persecution which occurred immediately after the stoning of Stephen (Acts 8), Paul had been commissioned by the Sanhedrin to locate and bring these "wayward" Jews back.

Paul had been given the proper papers to retain and imprison those Jewish people who had (in his opinion) wandered from the faith of Judaism to the faith of Christianity. In fact, Paul's authority to detain and arrest *only* extended to Jewish people. It did *not* extend to Gentiles. For Paul to have had the authority to hunt down Gentiles, he would have had to obtain written permission from the Roman government. Of course, the Roman government would have given no such permission for a Jew to hunt down Roman citizens, and Paul would have been arrested and imprisoned for such actions. Nonetheless, Paul did *not* have this authority, simply because he was not interested in tracking down Gentiles who had converted to Christianity. As a Jewish Pharisee, that would not have been within the scope of his mission or responsibility.

Paul also spends a good portion of Galatians chapters one and two proving the authenticity of his apostleship. Why did he take the time to do this? It is obvious that the Judaizers attempted to cast doubt on Paul's *credentials*. They attempted to *undermine* his ministry and his authority. If they could successfully accomplish this, they would have the upper hand in gaining the favor of the Jewish believers in the churches of Galatia. This would then become the catalyst for bringing these errant Jewish believers back into the fold of Judaism.

The entire issue at stake in the letter to the Galatians can be summed up in one word: **salvation**! Paul speaks a great deal on this subject throughout Galatians. He is constantly comparing and contrasting the Law given through Moses with the freedom purchased through Christ with respect to salvation, the part of the Abrahamic Covenant that applies to *all people*, regardless of race or gender.

Circumcision is the covenant sign between the Jewish people of Israel and God. To Judaizers, it was this particular sign that meant the difference between receiving salvation and not receiving it. Without circumcision, it was impossible to have God's salvation, because He was not approachable without it. So it naturally comes up in Paul's letter because these Judaizers (being *Jewish*) saw their fellow Jews as people who had *left* Judaism and therefore, had left God Himself. This is why Paul seems to understand their zeal, yet he also condemns this same zeal because it is misplaced.

It is very important to understand that any Judaizers who might have been moving from church to church, attempting to undo Paul's work, would have no interest in *Gentiles* and whether they were circumcised or not. Their concern extended to *Jewish converts* only. This is the way it is today as well. If you speak with orthodox Jews, they will proudly tell you that they do not proselytize. Their concern has always been with those within the house of Israel, not those outside Israel.

Why is all of this information so important? Because if we understand that Paul's letter was *primarily* to Jewish believers, the entire letter to the Galatians takes on a completely different meaning – one in which God intended it to have. This is why context is so extremely important. Galatians is a letter from Paul in which he *is* speaking principally to Jewish brethren. As the apostle to the Gentiles, he would not have been worried about Judaizers going after the Gentiles, but only Jewish believers!

In 2:16ff, Paul states, "*We ourselves are Jews by birth and not Gentile sinners; yet we know that a person is not justified by works of the law but through faith in Jesus Christ*" (Galatians 2:15-16; ESV).

Notice that Paul says "we," indicating that he is including himself as he talks with people who were also Jewish. Paul also *differentiates* between Jews and Gentiles, though he soon speaks of the fact that all differences between men and women, slave and free, Jew and Gentile have been *eradicated*. Is Paul contradicting himself?

We know from Acts 13 and following that wherever Paul went to preach the gospel, he went to the synagogues first. He was normally heard, at least initially, until some Jewish individuals decided he was preaching heresy. Though many Jewish people received the gospel, it was because of this that he was normally chased out of town, or worse. He would *then* take his message of the gospel to the Gentiles.

While there were undoubtedly Gentiles in these young churches which had been established through Paul and Barnabas' ministry, the fact that these churches were made up of largely Jewish converts cannot be ignored or denied. This is the sole reason why Paul refers to the Old Testament so often! The Jewish people he was writing to would have been very familiar with the Old Testament and with Abraham. They would have also understood exactly what he was talking about. Not so with the Gentiles. He would have been wasting his words on them, since they would have been unfamiliar with the teachings of the OT. Greeks (Gentiles) would not have known the specifics of the Abrahamic Covenant, for example, nor would they have cared, since it was not part of their cultural heritage.

In chapter three, Paul states, "*Know then that it is those of faith who are the sons of Abraham. And the Scripture, foreseeing that God would justify the Gentiles by faith, preached the gospel beforehand to Abraham, saying, 'In you shall all the nations be blessed.' So then, those who are of faith are blessed along with Abraham, the man of faith*" (Galatians 3:7-9; ESV). Please note that Paul is speaking *about* Jews here, whom he calls "the sons of Abraham" (those of faith). He *then* speaks about Gentiles, pointing out that the gospel would be extended to them as well. Later in this same chapter, Paul teaches that the Abrahamic Covenant is still being upheld *through* Christ, not negated.

In chapter three, beginning with verse 28, Paul states, "*There is neither Jew nor Greek, there is neither slave nor free, there is no male and female, for you are all one in Christ Jesus. And if you are Christ's, then you are Abraham's offspring, heirs according to promise*" (Galatians 3:28-29; ESV).

What does "*heirs according to promise*" mean? We know that the *entirety* of Galatians is dealing with the subject of *salvation*. Paul is dealing with *no other* aspect of the Abrahamic Covenant. He is dealing *only* with *salvation*, and does so by comparing the Law with Grace, slave with free. Salvation is now extended through Christ to all nations and all people. Israel has been *temporarily* set aside (as we learn in Romans 9-11) in order for this to occur.

If Israel was set aside temporarily, there must be an *end* to this *setting aside*, because the very word "*temporarily*" implies a beginning and an ending. If God has set Israel aside for a time, we must ask, *from what* is God setting them aside? There must be something He is *not* doing with them, though He is obviously *still* saving individual Jewish people. Paul is proof of that, as is Barnabas, and others.

What is God *not* doing with Israel now that He was doing *before* they rejected Christ? There are only two things that God is *not* doing with the Jewish people *now*:

1. *He is not working with Israel as a nation.*
2. *He is not fulfilling all aspects of the Abrahamic Covenant, aside from salvation.*

These are the only logical conclusions that can be arrived at while maintaining the integrity of Scripture. God must have obviously placed aspects of the Abrahamic Covenant *on hold,* and if they are on hold temporarily, then at some point in time God will *lift* this temporary hold, to once again deal with Israel as a nation. Do we have any idea when this temporary hold that God has placed on Israel will expire? Yes, we do, and it is also in Romans 9-11.

If God had *not* set Israel aside, He would be required to extend the gospel message to the Gentiles *through* the nation of Israel, as He did in the Old Testament. Since the nation of Israel rejected Christ, God rejected Israel, but as stated, *only* temporarily.

Returning to Galatians 5, we note that Paul is *still* speaking about *circumcision*, which to orthodox Jews would have been a sign of salvation. It becomes obvious that there were *Jewish believers* in the churches in Galatia who were being told that though they were Christian, they *still* needed to be circumcised, or their covenant with God would be made null and void. This in turn (the Judaizers believed) would affect the *entire* nation of Israel, since God always dealt with Israel as a *whole*.

Even toward the end of chapter six, Paul *continues* speaking concerning circumcision. When he closes with the phrase "the Israel of God," he is speaking about the Remnant, who came from *within* the nation of Israel. During his day, Paul was part of the Remnant for that generation.

If a distinction between Jews and Gentiles is *not understood in Galatians,* the understanding will be wrong, in spite of Paul's comments regarding the lack of distinction between male, female, etc. If people do not realize that Paul is speaking mainly *to* Jews, who were in the various churches of Galatia, they will misunderstand Paul's teaching, as many have done and continue to do today!

What of the Distinctions?
Theodore Pike understands the Galatians 3:28-29 passage to be a text proving that all ethnic and gender distinctions have been erased *now.* Alan Nairne believes the same thing, stating, *"Paul writing to both the Ephesian Christians (Eph.2:11-22) and those at Colossae (3:10-11) makes it clear that racial and national distinctions are forever gone."*[28]

Paul clearly states that this is the case, but what does he mean? This is where some might say that I should be taking things literally. I plan to do just that, as soon as I know what Paul *means* in this section. When I speak of understanding the Bible in *literal* terms, I am *always* referring to interpreting the Bible with its literal *meaning.* In order for me to do that, I must know everything I can know about the passage, including the context. All of this together allows me to literally understand what Paul is actually *stating*.

Most commentators believe that Paul wrote Galatians before he wrote any other book. If this is so, then why does Paul takes pains to tell Timothy that there are rules for men and women in church in 1 Timothy 2:12-13, which came *after* Galatians? Beyond this, Paul (and Peter) spends a good amount of time discussing the roles in marriage (cf. Ephesians 5:21-25; Colossians 3:18-19; 1 Peter 3:1-7). How

---

[28] http://www.apocalipsis.org/Israel.htm

could this be, if Paul was *really* teaching that all ethnic and gender distinctions are gone? Is Paul contradicting himself here?

It should be obvious that Paul is referring to the fact that *in Christ* – meaning in the *spiritual* realm – we are *one* because we *are* the perfected Bride of Christ in the spiritual realm. Essentially, in eternity, at the marriage of the Lamb, all within the Church will represent the *one* Bride. At that point, it is plain that all gender, racial and positional distinctions are gone.

In reality, this does not happen as long as the Bride of Christ remains on this earth. I'm not perfect! I have not reached a state of sinless perfection and neither has any other Christian still alive. It will only be when I see my Savior face to face that I will be like Him (cf. 1 John 3:2). Beyond this, of course, while the Bride of Christ is *one* in Him, some members of the Bride are currently with Him while others are here on earth, and there may be some who have not been born yet.

Paul is *not* teaching that *here on earth* all distinctions no longer exist. If that is what he was saying, then he *would* obviously be contradicting himself later in other books. He cannot be stating that here on earth, in our *imperfect* vessels of clay, all distinctions have been set aside now.

Since the entire letter to the Galatian churches deals with *salvation*, it should be apparent that Paul is teaching that as far as *salvation* is concerned, there is *no* difference between people. It does not matter if someone is a *king* or a *slave*, a *man* or a *woman*, a *Jewish* individual or a *Gentile* person. In each case, *all* people have the very same ability to receive salvation from the hand of Christ *without distinction*. This is what Paul is teaching. Salvation is for *all* people, irrespective of gender, race, or position in life. Paul is *not* teaching that these distinctions are removed while we are here in this life. He *supports* some of these distinctions to the letters to Titus and Timothy. To Philemon, he never stated that he should set Onesimus *free*, because Onesimus was already free in Christ! Moreover, throughout the book of Acts, even *after* Paul wrote his letter to the Galatian churches, he continued to go to the Jewish synagogues, offering the gospel to the Jews first, and *then* to the Gentiles, thereby placing the Jewish person first. Again, if he was teaching that all distinctions are now gone, then he would be hypocritically practicing what he did not preach. Paul did not do that.

If Paul had seriously *meant* that all distinctions had been removed, he would have preached the gospel to all people regardless of their ethnicity, position or gender. It is clear, though, that Paul does not do that. He continues to maintain a distinction between Jews and Gentiles.

Paul says something which is similar to this in his letter to the Ephesians, written circa late 50s A.D., some ten or so years *after* he composed his letter to the Galatian churches. He makes this statement: *"God, being rich in mercy, because of the great love with which he loved us, even when we were dead in our trespasses, made us alive together with Christ— by grace you have been saved— and raised us up with him and seated us with him in the heavenly places in Christ Jesus"* (Ephesians 2:4-6).

This is another spiritual truth that must be analyzed in order to know exactly what Paul means. Paul is saying that right now, every Christian is seated with Christ in the heavenlies. However, *that* means that in the *spiritual* realm, all Christians are already with Christ. We are as good as *there,* because God sees us there already. Paul must be referring to the spiritual realm, because physically, Christians alive now are not in heaven. In fact, it is our physical bodies that keep our spirits tied to the earth! Paul seems to be saying that *because* our spirits are already seated with our Lord Jesus Christ, we benefit from that as we live the remainder of our lives here, *on earth.* Through the Holy Spirit, our spirits are already seated with

Christ. This is part of the guarantee that we *will* be with Christ physically *after* we die.

While we are unable to know and experience the full force of the blessing of actually *being* with Christ physically *now*, our spirit benefits greatly from our spiritual union with Him in this life. Certainly, aspects of that truth impact our attitude and demeanor *here* and *now*. Our life here on earth is blessed by our spirit's association with Christ now. We grow, mature and become more like Christ because of it. However, *after* we die we will enjoy the *full* benefits of our union with Christ.

Paul often referred to things in the spiritual realm that we cannot see and certainly cannot fully appreciate. Nonetheless, these spiritual blessings and benefits are real, and we profit from them. When we reach heaven with Christ, the *entire Body* we call the Church will at that point be completely united into *one,* with absolutely *no* distinction between ethnicity, position or gender.

This is clearly *not* the case now as we live within our physical tents here, and Paul is not teaching otherwise. He is *not* teaching that all distinctions are gone now, nor is he teaching that *everything* that was promised to Abraham's seed has been *fulfilled in the Church.* This is plain, because all of what he discusses in his letter to the Galatian churches has to do with *salvation.* He does *not* discuss the land, nor does he discuss any other portion of the Abrahamic Covenant.

Anti-Semitism Securely In Place

Regarding the error of Replacement Theology, one of the websites we quoted from earlier says this about Anti-Semitism within the Church: *"Unfortunately the Church, being more concerned with her own interests, has failed historically to heed these clear warnings and the result has been arrogance, pride and anti-Semitism. There is a clear link between anti-Semitism and the Church over the centuries of history, and Replacement Theology has made a major contribution to this evil."*[29]

It is not at all difficult to see how insidious this form of Anti-Semitism has become. In many articles and books, the position is usually established that all should be defended *except* the Jewish person. The amount of anger, vitriol and contempt for Jews, as well as those who support them, is readily seen in what these individuals say, write and advocate.

Returning to the very first person we quoted from, Carol A. Valentine, we see that this comment of hers bears further consideration: *"Read the Book of Joshua if you don't believe this."* Here, she has just finished commenting on the "mean-spirited Jehovah" playing favorites with the nation of Israel and the unspeakable atrocities they committed in His Name. Then she points us to the book of Joshua.

What I am assuming Valentine is implying is that what the Jews did after they entered the Promised Land was blatantly *wrong*. This is in spite of the fact God instructed them to go into the Land of Canaan and deal with the people who lived there as *His arm of judgment*. It is clear that Valentine's difficulty lies in the fact that the Jews were commanded to rid the land of *Gentiles*. So her point seems to be that the Jews have *always* gone after the Gentiles.

In believing that what the Jews perpetrated against Gentiles was wrong, Valentine apparently considers the actions of the Jewish people to be *racist*. She of necessity disagrees with Scripture, which states that what Israel did was done by order of God. This is extremely ironic, since she obviously does not see her own anti-Semitism, yet can point to racist tendencies and actions *from* Jew *toward* Gentile.

---

[29] http://christianactionforisrael.org/4thcongress2.html

Killing Them All in Canaan

Whether Valentine or anyone else believes that what Israel did was due to God's commands is beside the point. Scripture indicates that God had some very good reasons to use Israel as His arm of judgment against the nations that lived in the Promised Land. If we look at the text in both Numbers and Joshua, clearly the land had *giants* in it. This same word appears in Genesis 6 where we are told that giants existed in the world in those days. These giants were very powerful individuals, not merely in strength, but in mental ability as well.

It is believed by many commentators that these giants, known as Nephilim, existed as the result of fornication between *fallen angels* and human women. How that actually took place is not known (and certainly some things are better not known). It seems that the text which says, *"the sons of God saw the daughters of men, that they were beautiful; and they took wives for themselves of all whom they chose"* (Genesis 6:2) indicates an intermingling.[30]

From this intermingling, a human-hybrid race was "created" which, if successful, would eventually corrupt the entire human DNA. This mutated offspring was the largest reason why God had to destroy the ancient world, saving only Noah and his family. Apparently, Noah and his family had not had their DNA corrupted by any unions with angelic beings, according to Genesis 6.

When Moses and the children of Israel first arrived at the borders of the Land of Canaan, they saw these giants (cf. Numbers 13; also Deuteronomy 1). These giants were what caused the fear to rise in many within the nation of Israel.

---

[30] The phrase "sons of God" is normally understood to mean angelic beings for a number of reasons. It is not my purpose to argue for or against the Sethian lineage as being a candidate for "sons of God." There are plenty of books and articles that have already been written on that subject. Suffice it to say that I am satisfied that there was an actual co-mingling between fallen angel and human being, producing the hybrid race, Nephilim.

God had always planned to use His nation of Israel as both a light to the world and an arm of judgment against other nations who were in rebellion against Him through idolatry or some other evil. This was the case as Israel prepared to enter Canaan. They were supposed to completely *wipe out* and destroy all people because the Nephilim line had obviously made a comeback since the days of Noah. Given that this was the case, there was a very distinct danger that it had infected every aspect of the people who already lived in Canaan. Nothing was to remain alive.

When the Nephilim were destroyed in the global flood, their bodies died, but not their spirits. Their spirits would roam around trying to find other physical bodies to live in, and this could well extend to the animal kingdom. We have an excellent example of this in Christ's day. When He cast out the demoniac at Gadarenes, He allowed the demons – named *Legion* – to inhabit the herd of swine nearby. Apparently, these spirits hate not having a body in which to dwell (cf. Matt 8; Mark 5; Luke 8). Because of their ability to possess and infect with evil, God had every reason and right to use Israel as His physical arm of judgment against these nations as they entered His land.

However, even when the children of Israel did enter the Land after wandering for forty years, they still did not do what God wanted. Because of that, the Philistines, as one example, continued to live in the land. It was not until a number of generations later that David went against Goliath, who was said to be roughly nine feet, six inches tall, and he was considered the smaller of his brothers!

We can play armchair quarterback and believe that Israel's aggression was reprehensible, but the truth of the matter is that they were under direct orders from God. Moses makes this abundantly clear toward the end of the book of Numbers. So to *reprimand* Israel for their actions is to reprimand *God*.

At least part of the reason for God's direction to destroy these people had to do with the corruption of the human race through the introduction of this hybrid species (angel and human), both before and after the global flood. Even though God dealt with this first occurrence with the global flood, it appears that they began to rise up again and were already *waiting* for Israel by the time they reached Canaan. It is clear then that Satan had been busy for centuries attempting to thwart God's plans once again where Israel is concerned.

In light of today's teachings espoused by Replacement Theology and Preterism, it is becoming increasingly clear that the position of Anti-Zionism seems to have its origin in the same source as the one who has attempted to destroy God's plans from the beginning; Satan himself. However, Satan's modus operandi is to use these individuals to viciously attack the Christian Zionist for advocating support for Israel's future.

Of course, the Replacement Theologian bristles at the suggestion that the view they hold may, in fact, be Anti-Semitic. The possibility *must* be considered and investigated.

12

Replacement?

Replacement Theology (as well as Covenant Theology and Preterism), postulates that Israel has been *replaced* by the Church. Therefore, Israel exists no more, they say. She is gone, history, kaput. Because Israel rejected her Messiah, ultimately crucifying Him, God's patience had run out (their view), and due to this, He utterly and permanently broke fellowship with Israel, casting them aside. In this author's opinion, the eyes of the individuals who believe this remain closed to the truth. They seem unable or unwilling (or maybe both) to hear what Gabriel has clearly stated to Daniel.

This is an unfortunate position to accept as true, because as mentioned, it appears to be completely *unbiblical*. There is really nothing in Scripture (if Scripture is allowed to speak for itself) that lends support to this current and errant view of God's dealings with either the Church or Israel.

If we consider all the times that Israel utterly failed God by refusing to believe Him, which led to rebellion and disobedience, we *never* see a time when God cast Israel away from Himself *permanently*. God always emphasized His faithfulness in spite of Israel's disobedience. Yet we are to now believe that God finally came to a point of realizing that continuing with Israel was hopeless, so He abandoned them, creating a new entity instead in which there would be no difference between the Jew or Gentile, man or woman, free or slave.

God, the Breaker of Promises
Unfortunately, it appears that this view tends to make God one who reneges on His promises. In this case, the promises were stated to Abraham not once, but on at least three separate occasions, and then to others who came after Abraham as well.

Theologians who believe that God tossed Israel aside do so based on Israel's rejection of Jesus as Messiah. However, it is clear from the Old Testament alone that the Messiah was to be rejected and would die as a direct result of that rejection. Since God saw, knew and even designed this to occur, it is difficult to believe that this rejection of Christ was God's "final straw." This is especially difficult to grasp considering the fact that God made the specific promises to Abraham that were unconditional (though the Covenant Theologian views these as *conditional* promises). Clearly, the Gentiles would benefit (all the families of the earth will be blessed through Abraham; Genesis 12:1-3), and this benefit refers to *salvation*. The other promises made to Abraham were specifically made for the future nation of Israel and cannot, nor should be, transferred to the Church.

Isaiah 53, Daniel 9 and numerous other portions of Scripture clearly indicate that the Messiah was to be killed long before it happened.

We will also note that every time Israel rejected God in some way or form, His judgment always came. This was the reason Israel (the southern kingdom) was in captivity in Babylon in the book of Daniel. Israel had rejected God, refusing to comply with His rule over them.

Every time Israel rejects God through some form of rebellion, God sends judgment. This is usually accomplished by activating a neighboring empire, who would sweep in, destroying much of Israel's population. Any remaining Israelites would be taken alive as slaves. This happened time and time again. Israel was normally tossed or carried out of the Land they possessed. Israelites were dispersed into the world among their captives and foreign nations.

Eventually, God always brought them back to their own Land and to the city of Jerusalem, God's center of the world. There is no reason to believe that God always intended to, at one point, drop Israel forever. In fact, Scripture seems to indicate otherwise.

One Rejection After Another
Israel's path has always been a series of obedience to God and then rejection of Him. From there, Israel would be overcome by a foreign entity, taken captive and led out of the Land. After a time, they cried out to God (usually a new generation of Jews), and God would open His ears. He then rescues Israel from her captives, bringing her back to her homeland. That is the cycle, and in essence, they are in a "dispersion" part of that cycle now, though we can see throughout the world that since 1948 Jewish people have begun making their way back to Israel. However, in this current case, it is noteworthy to understand that though this author believes God is responsible for bringing them back to the land, the Israelites themselves are unaware of it. They have not called out to Him. They are merely being brought back to the Land (cf. Ezekiel 20) for God's purposes.

It is important to note, too, that every time Israel needed to be judged by God, it was based on the fact that God had been *rejected* as King over Israel. This was first done by the Israelites demanding to have a human king over themselves, and resulted in the ordination of Saul to that office, the first of many kings (cf. 1 Samuel). God knew they were rejecting Him and His rule.

Every time judgment occurred with Israel, it occurred because of their rejection of God. It did not matter if it was because of specific idolatry or by rejecting other laws that God had given to the nation. All of it resulted in Israel's rejection of God. This is what it all came down to for them.

The same is true during Jesus' time. He appeared on this planet in the form of a baby, grew up among His own Jewish people, ministered to them for roughly three years, and was, with finality, rejected by the religious leaders of Israel. He was then executed by crucifixion. This rejection of God was happening again in the cycle. Israel's leaders were *rejecting* God. There is nothing new here at all. It was always the same type of rejection.

In spite of this, many would have us believe that this rejection of Jesus was something so horrendous that it caused the nation of Israel to go beyond God's ability to forgive. This left God with no choice but to permanently cast Israel off as the favored nation.

This is absolute nonsense, as Israel *always* rejected God in one form or another when it came to that part of the cycle. We are to believe that this particular act of rejecting God in Jesus somehow pushed God over the edge? We are to believe that God looked at Israel and said, *"All those times in the past, rejecting my commands, my love, they were rejecting Me as Ruler over them. This final time, they have rejected my commands, my love, and Me as Ruler (through my Son). That's it! I've had it with Israel! I will forget them forever!"*

While the Anti-Zionist wishes us to believe that this rejection of Jesus Christ was so dire that it trumped any and all of the prior rejections of God, the truth of the matter is that *all* rejections of God by Israel were the same: *rejection of God*. There is *no* difference. Rejecting God is rejecting *God*. There are not *degrees* to rejecting God. A person does not reject God just a little, or quite a lot. Rejecting God is rejecting God.

The Birth of Replacement Theology

At this point, a few more comments from the Christian Action for Israel's website are in order. *"One of the factors that led to the birth of Replacement Theology was an historic one. This teaching was birthed at a time when Israel as a nation was in dispersion. The Land of Canaan was barren, infertile and her cities, especially Jerusalem, were mere desert outposts. The devastation was complete and it seemed beyond belief that the Land could ever again be restored to its former glory.*

"The impossibility of the situation led to a false re-interpretation of God's Word. Christendom has since paid the price. For God confounded her unbelief in 1948 with the restoration of the State of Israel and exposed the tragic and wicked fruits of Replacement Theology. Christian Zionists are determined to proclaim the truth of the New Testament, namely that God is not finished with Israel and that, in fact, she will yet become a 'cornerstone' of His plan for the world.

"Thirdly, Christian Zionists recognise with sorrow and repentance the role that many Christians have played in the persecution of the Jewish People. This is even more disturbing since all we love and enjoy as Christians came from them (Romans 9:1-5). In the light of this awful reality they seek to be a blessing and source of comfort to Zion (Isaiah 40:1-2)."[31]

A Bit of History

History has shown that many within Christendom viewed the 1948

---

[31] http://christianactionforisrael.org/4thcongress2.html

event of Israel's statehood with shock and incredulity. It nowhere fits *their* understanding of God's dealings with Israel. Because they firmly believed then (and now) that Israel was entirely and permanently rejected *by* God, the fact that she is now a state can be nothing more than an accident of nature.

If not for the United Nations (we are told by Anti-Zionists), Israel would not have had a chance to gain her current statehood. Because of this aid, the United Nations is guilty of forcing untold thousands of Arabs to deal with "their" land being given away with a "take it or leave it" ultimatum.

Anti-Zionists are convinced that the continued unrest in the Middle East today is due *solely* to Israel's presence. The Jewish people have *no* business being there as a state again. If they just went there to live, that would be one thing, but they went there to live *and* to become a sovereign state. This was the catalyst that created unrest and untold difficulties for Arabs because of Israel's aggression. These are the arguments we hear over and over.

It is absolutely true that the Land of Canaan in 1948 was, in large measure, completely desolate. Nothing was growing, and dirt and dust went on for miles and miles. Any Arabs who *did* live there existed as Bedouins, with their families and herds moving from place to place as the weather and seasons dictated in order to survive.

Once Jewish people began relocating back to Israel, however, things began to change. The once barren and desolate fields and valleys were transformed into gardens of oases everywhere. Kibbutzim sprang up here and there. There were no walls to protect these new communities. When they took up residence, the Jewish people *changed* the land as if God's blessing was once again upon them.

This needs to be understood. Israel as a land was essentially lying vacant, and it was not until the people of Israel began to relocate to it and renovate many areas within Israel that suddenly it became something that Arabs wanted for themselves.

Yasser Arafat also took advantage of the situation by artificially *creating* a culture of Arab people he called *Palestinians*. Prior to this PR campaign of Arafat's, *anyone* and *everyone* who lived in that area was referred to as Palestinian. This applied to Jews as well as Arabs and other Gentiles.

Yessir Yasser

Yasser Arafat was successful in singling out Arabs as if *they* were the only ones to rightly be called Palestinian. This gave them a decided advantage because it began to appear to the world that these Arabs – now Palestinians – were already well ensconced in that geographical area. It began to appear as though the Jews, who were now coming back to Canaan in large numbers, were, in fact, *displacing* people who actually *belonged* there. This was not true, though.

It would be helpful at this juncture to discover what the apostle Paul teaches about Israel and whether or not there is any possibility of a future for them as a nation.

As we have discussed, it is known from the book of Acts that Paul (*Saul* prior to his salvation) met Christ on the road to Damascus (cf. Acts 9). He was on a mission sanctioned by the religious leaders of Israel to chase down and bring back (or have executed) any Jews who had become followers of "The Way" (a derogatory term for Christianity at that time in history). This is what Paul was in the process of accomplishing as he headed toward Damascus.

When Paul's life was transformed by Jesus on that road, he not only became a follower of Him, but completely dedicated his life from that moment on to evangelizing the lost, starting with Jewish people. The lost, as far as Paul was concerned, were found in the Jews of Israel. He also realized that the gospel was to go out to the Gentiles as well, and it was in this order that he presented the gospel: to the Jew first and also to the Gentile. Though some try to argue otherwise, Paul never varied his methods.

It is clear from a number of statements Paul makes that his knowledge of Jesus Christ came directly from Jesus Himself. This form of revelation was special to Paul, as it should be. He claimed he built on no one else's ministry and even what he was taught came directly from Jesus, not from any of the other apostles (Galatians 1:12; 2:2). It was because of his tremendous understanding of Scripture (the Old Testament, or T'nach) that Jesus taught and revealed to Paul the truths *behind* the text, of which many ultimately referred to Him as Messiah.

This divine revelation was the foundational basis for his ministry. With respect to God's revelations to Paul, it was Paul who first spoke of the Church as being a mystery (cf. Romans 16:25; Galatians 3:23; Ephesians 3:3, 5). It is clear from Paul's teaching that nothing like the Church was known prior to Christ.

Replacement Theology in the Batter's Box
Replacement Theology has an interesting (albeit wrong) way of getting around this. They say that God had *always* meant for the gospel to be extended to the Gentiles, therefore it was not a true mystery, since it was known from the Old Testament that the gospel would always go out to the Gentiles. However, the mystery that Paul spoke of was in making the "two men one," which is what occurs during the regeneration process alike for Jews and Gentiles. This is nowhere to be found in the Old Testament, or prior to Paul revealing it, for that matter.

I know of no one who denies that the Old Testament teaches that the gospel was to be extended to the Gentiles. Unfortunately, though, Anti-Zionists are confusing the fact that the gospel would extend to the Gentiles with the creation of the Church. Paul is speaking specifically of the Church, or the Bride of Christ, that would include people of all cultures and nations and was completely separate from the nation of Israel. This entity was *nowhere* indicated in the Old Testament.

The fact that we see from the Old Testament that the gospel *would* be extended to the Gentiles does *not* mean that the Old Testament prophets knew of the *eventual* establishment of the Church. They most likely understood that the gospel would be extended to the Gentiles *through* the nation of Israel.

There was actually no reason for God to reveal this aspect of His plan to the prophets of the OT, and for one extremely good reason: Had God revealed any aspect of the Church, or even *hinted* at it in the Old Testament, that knowledge would have *also been* revealed to *Satan*. Had Satan known about the Church, it is extremely likely that he would have done things markedly different before and during the lifetime of Christ on earth.

Satan was obviously aware of Jesus' birth from the Old Testament Scriptures, and he also knew where that birth would take place. He attempted to work through Herod to accomplish his ends of destroying Christ before He could grow up and go to the cross. Instead, an untold number of innocent babies were brutally murdered by Roman soldiers. Numerous times throughout Christ's earthly life, Satan attempted to incite the religious leaders of Israel to kill Jesus, which would have been ahead of His time.

Had Satan known about the Church, he most assuredly would have done all he could to have stopped Christ from being crucified. Knowledge of the Church would have given him knowledge of many other things. Putting two and two together, Satan could have mounted a major campaign against the Church prior to its inception. Certainly, he would have tried to stop it. As it was (and is), he had to make due with his consant attempts of introducing error into the Church.

God kept the mystery of the Church all to Himself. This group of believers taken from all nations and cultures makes up one Body – one Bride, for Jesus Christ.

So while the Anti-Zionist believes, and diligently argues, that the Church was known in the Old Testament, Scripture proves otherwise. Had it not been a real *mystery*, Paul would never have referred to it as such. While we know (from the OT) that the gospel was to go out to the Gentiles, there is nothing there which teaches or explains the *essence* of the Church; the idea of all being made complete in Christ with no differentiation between gender or ethnicity *is* the Church.

But what else does the Anti-Zionist believe that conflicts with biblical authority? Just as importantly, where did these particular views and teachings start?

Origen
For most students of church history, just mentioning the name *Origen* is enough to provide the answer. Most know of his proclivity to allegorize, and he was possibly one of the most educated men of the early Church fathers.

History tells us that he was born in Alexandria around A.D. 186 and died in A.D. 254. Most of the documents he composed were written between the years A.D. 204 to 232.

Because of Alexander the Great and due to its literature, the city of Alexandria had become the main seat of Greek learning. The Greek influence had spread over the known world. *"It was also the chief seat of Christian theology until it was taken over by Arabs in 641 A.D."*[32]

Origen was a tremendous scholar and writer. The main problem, though, was his method of interpretation (if it can be called that). He believed that *"scripture admits of a three-fold interpretation corresponding to the tripartite nature of man: the 'bodily' (the literal or historical); the 'psychical' (the ethical); and the 'pneumatic' (the allegorical or mystical)."*[33] So, here we have a deeply committed man of faith who had apparently worked out a system of theology that was so convoluted, even he became confused at times!

Many scholars and commentators who came well after Origen did not speak highly of him. In one particular writing related to Israel, Origen states without equivocation, *"We may thus assert in utter confidence that the Jews will not return to their earlier situation, for they have committed the most abominable of crimes in forming this conspiracy against the Savior of the human race..."*[34]

For Origen, and those who believe as he did, it is no secret that the A.D. 70 destruction of Jerusalem was the direct result of Israel's rejection of Christ. However, *that* was the judgment, along with being once again dispersed. There is nothing in the Olivet Discourse indicating that the Jews would never return to the Land to possess it. The only way this can be understood from Scripture is by allegorizing various biblical texts. More often than not, Scripture is allegorized by the *interpreter's* choice, not because the text actually insists upon it.

People like to point out that if something is fairly new in development (further away from the beginnings of the Church), then

---

[32] Derek White, *Replacement Theology: Its Origin, History and Theology* (East Sussex: CFI Communications 1997), 5
[33] Ibid, 6
[34] Ibid, 6-7

it should be avoided. This is the constant mantra against Dispensationalism; that it is supposedly new, having begun with Darby. This is not really the case, but no one is really paying attention, irrespective of how much factual information is supplied for them. There are a number of biblical doctrines that were dormant for many centuries, only coming once again to light during and after the Reformation. No one complains about these doctrines, though.

Be that as it may, in the case of Origen, we have an individual who was very close to the first century churches, yet came up with a system of interpretation that is plainly absurd! The system he developed must be avoided if for no other reason than the fact that the interpreter becomes the subjective source of truth revealed in Scripture.

Development of Replacement Theology

It is very easy to see how this Replacement Theology came into development. By the second century, the Church was left trying to determine its identity, since it was made up of both Jews and Gentiles by this point. In some areas, it created a major identity crisis, and the answer was determined to be in what Origen had stated, which became known as Replacement Theology.

Augustine carried the idea forward and it became an integral part of Roman Catholic doctrine. This theology prompted an attitude of blame toward the Jews as individuals and as a people group. From this point on, the covenant in Jeremiah 31 was seen to *exclude* Jews. Upon searching the writings of the Church fathers from this era of time, it is exceedingly rare to find even reference to Paul's teaching on the ultimate redemption of Israel. Just because this belief of the early Church fathers was so prevalent, it does not make it a correct belief.

The Church had become the new Israel. All the blessings that were previously given *to* Israel were now applied to, and appropriated by, the Church. It was not long before the total culture of Judaism was literally wiped entirely away from the Bible and from the Church itself.

In the end, then, two major concepts encapsulated Replacement Theology:

1. *"All the premises and encouragements provided in the Old Testament are exclusively the property of the Church, which is now the true 'Israel.'*
2. *Israel has been completely disinherited and excluded. Furthermore, the formerly 'good' elements of Judaism have become 'evil' since Christ's coming."*[35]

From that point onward, it became very easy to not only treat the Jews as if they were disinherited by God, but to actually *negate* them as if they had never even been God's chosen people at all.

Many early Church fathers displayed a clear disregard for the Jews, including Jerome, Ambrose, Augustine, and Chrysostom. The latter typified the hatred that had developed by that time with the statement, *"When it is clear that God hates (the Jew), it is the duty of Christians to hate them too."*[36]

In essence, this Replacement Theology is founded upon two things: 1) bad hermeneutics, leading to a wrong interpretation of Scripture, and 2) hatred for the Jew. Is it any wonder that this led to the sizeable amount of anti-Semitism that has occurred throughout history? The historical landscape is filled with events, incidents and

---

[35] Derek White, *Replacement Theology: Its Origin, History and Theology* (East Sussex: CFI Communications 1997), 8
[36] Ibid, 9

even ways of life in which the Jew has been vilified, made null and void and cursed.

All of this was deliberately perpetrated by the Roman Catholic Church, which officially came into existence toward the end of the third century. Their anti-Semitism was and remains obvious, with their inquisitions, crusades, pogroms and all the rest. Is it any wonder Jewish individuals like Rashi, having grown up with much of this, became an ardent defender of Judaism and the Jew, denouncing the atrocities committed against his people by those who called themselves Christian?!? Christians of all denominations should be ashamed, as there is no excuse for what has taken place in God's Name against Jewish people. Doctrinal positions such as Replacement Theology and Preterism simply provide a vehicle which continues the anti-Semitic rhetoric.

Even during and after the Reformation, Luther (though successfully distancing himself from the error of salvation by faith plus works) was unable to extricate himself from the anti-Semitic rancor he held for the Jew. This same anti-Semitism has been pointed out by many since then, to no real avail.

Without this history of anti-Semitic vehemence, it is doubtful that Hitler would have been able to do what he did. Too many Christians stood by either watching or ignoring the atrocities altogether. They literally buried their heads in the sand as millions of Jewish people were illegally incarcerated, then either gassed or burned to death! How is *any* of that Christian?

We could spend more time explaining how the Christian Church divorced herself completely from her Jewish roots, but it is likely that the picture has been made clear. Anti-Semitism is an extremely ugly part of the Church's history. It stands there until the end of time as an example of brutality that can be perpetrated on an innocent people. The Church should be ashamed, and those who are not, while referring to themselves as Christian, are as guilty as those who did the deeds. The saddest part of all this is that anti-Semitism continues to exist through people like the Anti-Zionist, who sees no need for Jews or Israel. Because of that terrible deed of rejecting Christ and sending Him to His crucifixion, there is absolutely no forgiveness for the Jew or Israel, we are told by the Anti-Zionist.

Unfortunately, at the same time the Anti-Zionist is telling us that the Jew is "past tense," as is Israel, they are busy accusing the Christian Zionist of *excusing* the Jew for crucifying Christ. In essence, the Christian Zionist is made to appear as though he is aiding and abetting the Jew in this crime of murdering Jesus.

Both Jews AND Gentiles Are Guilty!
Here is the actual reality that the Replacement Theologian, Covenant Theologian, and Anti-Zionist have completely missed. No one group is guilty of perpetrating the crime of murder against Jesus Christ. *Both* Jew *and* Gentile played a role in Christ's death. The fault does not lie exclusively with the Jew as the Anti-Zionist would have us believe.

Yes, it was the group of religious leaders of Jesus' day, called the Sanhedrin, who brought charges against Jesus. He, of course, was completely innocent of those charges, but no one (Jew or Gentile) rose to His defense. Since these religious leaders could not put Him to death themselves, they needed the government of Rome to do it, so they turned to Pontus Pilate.

Rome, through Pilate, originally wanted nothing to do with Jesus. Pilate knew that Jesus was not a threat to Roman rule. He found nothing evil in Him and relayed his findings to the religious leaders of Israel. Not satisfied with Pilate, they demanded that Jesus be crucified.

Even Pilate's wife warned her husband that he should have nothing to do with Christ's trial at all. He should have listened to her. Pilate – a Gentile – was the one who pronounced sentence, and to make matters worse, he had Christ scourged prior to the execution. While this was the custom, since Pilate knew that Christ was innocent of the charges, one has to wonder why he felt he needed to include scourging in the process. Yes, it was prophesied that Christ would suffer the pain and humiliation of scourging (cf. Isaiah 53). However, Pilate suffers the condemnation for going ahead with that decision.

The Roman soldiers (also Gentile) brutally scourged Christ after they tied him to the wooden post, completely stripping Him of His clothing. In all likelihood, there was one Roman soldier on each side of Christ, taking turns raining down the brutal beatings, one after the other. How many lashes Christ received is not clear, as much of it was left up to the sadism of the individual soldiers. When they grew tired, or bored, they would stop.

Once Christ had been thoroughly flogged, He was then roughly forced onto his back on the ground, with the crossbeam under His head. His hands would have been tied to the crossbeam. The upright stipe was already in the ground on Calvary's hill, silently and resolutely waiting for its next victim.

Once this was accomplished, Christ would be forced to walk nearly one full mile from Jerusalem to Calvary, just outside the city walls. We know from the gospels that He fell enough times during this trek to warrant someone else having to carry His crossbeam.

Arriving at Calvary, He would again be pushed backwards onto the ground. His arms would be spread into a 65 degree angle away from His body and His hands would be nailed to the crossbeam. This nailing was not done to ensure the body would remain on the cross, so much as it was done as an extra measure of sadism. The victim would often also have ropes tied around His arms to the crossbeam.

This is what actually kept the victim's wrists from falling off the cross.

Christ's feet were then nailed to the lower portion of the stipe; one foot over the other, so that only one nail was required. Of course, the victim was stripped completely of his clothes; another form of Roman indignity that the soldiers foisted upon their victims.

Once Christ's hands had been fully secured to the crossbeam, He would have then been hoisted up – one Roman soldier on each side – and because of the square hole in the center of the crossbeam, it would simply be placed over the upright stipe, sliding down until the thickness of the wood of the stipe kept it from sliding down further.

It was here, on the cross, that each victim would die. Pictures often depict Christ as being ten or more feet above the crowd. This was not the case. The Romans wanted things done quickly and efficiently. Getting Christ up to that height would have required ladders and a pulley system. Keeping the stipe's height so that it was essentially a little taller than an average man allowed the process to go very quickly. It also put the victim just above eye level with other individuals who would walk by. Because of this proximity, they could nearly look the victim directly in his eyes, face to face, and taunt him, spit on him, or slap him if they so desired. Crucifixion was an extremely brutal, humiliating way to be executed, and it was one of Rome's favorite techniques.

Let us not forget that, while the Jews brought their charges against Jesus to Pilate, it was the Gentile Pilate and the Gentile Roman soldiers who physically carried out the murder. If we want to consider people by ethnicity, then both Jews and Gentiles are guilty of murdering Jesus Christ. Fortunately for us, it was His death, the shedding of His blood and His resurrection that purchased salvation for us. Without His death, there would be no options. We would all ultimately face the second death in the Lake of Fire.

Ultimately, all those personally involved in that crucifixion process where Jesus is concerned bear the guilt, Jew and Gentile alike. However, it was for this that Christ came. His death was the price that needed to be paid, in order that we might become free of sin's punishment.

The Jews alone do not bear the guilt. It is spread equally among Jews and Gentiles, across the board. Those who firmly believe that the Jews alone are responsible for killing Christ do not know their Bible at all. However, it certainly appears as though they are all too familiar with racism in the form of Anti-Semitism, the result of which leads to Anti-Zionism every time.

Kingdom Now or Dominion Theology

"Perhaps the most extreme version of Replacement Theology is known as 'Kingdom Now' or 'Dominion Theology.' This teaches that the Church will govern the world and all its systems for Jesus. The Church will thus prepare the world for Him to step down from heaven and receive the reins of government from her."[37]

We see this theology unequivocally believed by many today. Christians are taught to believe they must be involved in social action issues. The more we can work to right all wrongs in society, the sooner Jesus will be able to return to this planet to reign. The emphasis here is on what *humanity* can accomplish. In other words, God's hands are tied, because He is in the position of having to wait while the Church on earth brings the entire earth, with the entire population, under the control or authority of the Church. Once this has been accomplished, then Jesus will be *able* to return to this world. This is exactly what Roman Catholicism attempted to do and failed.

---

[37] Derek White, *Replacement Theology: Its Origin, History and Theology* (East Sussex: CFI Communications 1997), 18

Replacement Theology Today
Today's Replacement Theology is very similar to its predecessor in the belief that all promises given to Israel are now to be appropriated by the Church. The chief means of seeing this is through the process of allegorizing Scripture and removing the literal aspect from it.

To the Replacement Theologian, then, this means that the Land of Israel, which God promised to be a possession to Israel *for all time,* is now meant to be the entire earth in which the Church obeys the Great Commission. It is taught that as more and more people come to a saving knowledge of Jesus Christ, more and more of the earth geographically comes under God's power and authority.

Isaiah 43:5-7, though referring to the regathering of Jews from all parts of the world, is now taken to mean the gathering of all *believers* in Christ from all parts of the world.

Hosea 6:1-2 discusses the future resurrection of Israel, yet for the Replacement Theologian it now refers to Jesus (the representative of Israel) having been raised from the dead. So instead of a physical resurrection of the Land of Israel with the Jews possessing it, it now refers to Jesus' resurrection and the future resurrection of those who believe in Him.

Beyond all of this, God specifically promised to David that someone from his house would sit on his throne and his throne would last forever (2 Samuel 7:13; 1 Chronicles 17:1-14). It is now taken to mean that the Church – now spiritual "Israel" – is ruled over by Jesus, the respresentative from Israel. He now sits on His Father's throne in heaven. He now rules over His people.

But there are some interesting thoughts hidden away from the Replacement Theologian's eyes in the Old Testament. When God made His pronouncement that someone from David's lineage would always sit on his throne, He followed through by providing a ruler from Solomon's branch of David's family for the next four hundred years. In Luke 1:32, in reference to Christ, it says that *"He will be great and will be called the Son of the Most High. And the Lord God will give to him the throne of his father David."*

There is a bit of a seeming parenthesis, though, after the four hundred years and prior to Christ's reign from his father David's throne. Anyone who knows the actual history of Israel as reported in God's Word knows that as time went on, the various kings over Israel had become so evil and corrupt that God had no choice but to remove them. Jeremiah 22:28-30 shows the extent of God's anger toward the line of kings. He decides that there will be no more kings from that line. The last king to reign over Israel was Jehoiachin, also called Jeconiah, and he only reigned for three months!

At first glance, it would appear as though God broke His promise to David. Yet this cannot be the case, since God cannot lie. So what happened? The Replacement theologian says that the promise was conditional and since Israel blew it, God was free to do as He pleased, no longer bound by the terms of the conditional covenant.

However, it seems clear enough that the promise made to David was actually *unconditional* in nature. This is plain enough from the same book of Jeremiah in which God cuts off the royal line to David's throne. Ten chapters after chapter twenty-two of Jeremiah, God says this to Jeremiah: *"For thus says the LORD: David shall never lack a man to sit on the throne of the house of Israel"* (Jeremiah 33:17). He says this *after* He states that there will be no more kings from the royal line in Jeremiah 22. If Scripture is allowed to interpret itself, there is only one feasible way to understand this; that God will continue with a king on David's physical throne. But how?

The evidence of Scripture supports the idea that God's promise to David was completely unconditional. The only "conditional" aspects of it might be seen in terms of each individual who sat on David's throne. Each could be removed as God saw fit, based on their loyalty to God. This, however, would in no way affect the unconditional promise that God had originally made to David.

Numbers 27:8 indicates how God worked after He chose to cut off the royal line from reigning. *"And you shall speak to the people of Israel, saying, 'If a man dies and has no son, then you shall transfer his inheritance to his daughter'."* Apparently, God chose to continue the royal line through daughters. Jack Kelly, of Grace Thru Faith, comments on this, stating, *"At the end of the Book of Numbers an interesting loophole emerged. A man died without a son, leaving [four] daughters. They came to Moses complaining that they would lose the family land since there was no son to inherit it. Moses sought the Lord, Who decreed that if there was no son in a family daughters could inherit family land providing they married within their own tribal clan. In effect they had to marry a cousin to keep the land 'in the family.' This made sense since land was allotted first by tribe then by clan then by family. Marrying within the clan kept the families in close proximity and preserved the tribal allotment. (Num. 36 1:13)"*[38]

What is extremely interesting about this is how the Lord worked out this scenario so that Jesus would be born of David's line, yet the "curse" God had placed on the royal line in Jeremiah 22 would not affect Christ because of the marriage of Joseph and Mary. Kelly explains, *"When Mary accepted Joseph's offer of marriage she preserved her family's land and also made good her son's claim to the throne of Israel... [Jesus was in the royal succession through Joseph but escaped the curse since he wasn't Joseph's biological son.] But He was a biological descendant of David's through his mother and therefore of the 'house and lineage of David'."*[39]

---

[38] http://gracethrufaith.com/childrens-stories-for-adults/the-virgin-mary-had-a-baby-boy/
[39] Ibid

Replacement Theology takes Old Testament passages that specifically reference Israel and the promises God made *to* them and repositions those passages so that they now point *to*, and find *fulfillment* in, the Church.

However, a close look at the text of Scripture and especially those repeated by Jesus during His earthly ministry clearly indicates that to Jesus, these were valid, as yet unfulfilled, promises that had been made to Israel. These *would* find their literal fulfillment at some point in future time through Christ physically. Jesus made no attempt to spiritualize or allegorize any of these passages of Scripture. He took them at face value, understanding them with a literal meaning.

A Multitude of Errors Within Replacement Theology
There are a number of glaring errors found within the system of Replacement Theology that need to be seen. These errors show that the Replacement Theologian, far from finding God's will and purposes in their method of interpretation, actually *changes* what God has clearly stated, making it say something else entirely. If this is the case, then the Replacement Theologian comes under judgment for sacrificing the actual meaning of God for the artificial meaning of man.

• **Law & Prophets Fulfilled By Jesus** – if, in fact, the Church is now the new Israel, then God has absolutely rejected Israel. This makes no sense in light of Christ's statement that He did not come to destroy the Law and Prophets, but to fulfill them (Matthew 5). He literally promises in Matthew 5 that nothing would pass away until *everything* (even the 'jot' and 'tittle' of Hebrew characters) came to pass.

• **"God has not rejected His people"** – Paul makes this abundantly clear in Romans 11. If God has, in fact, turned away permanently from Israel, why would Paul state that God has not done so? If the context means anything, Paul was undeniably referring to Israel here, not merely individual Jews. It seems obvious that Paul meant what he said, that God has not turned His back on His people.

• **Vindication** – one of the things Replacement Theologians seem to forget is that the major reason God will follow through on His promises is for the sake of His Name (Ezekiel 36, as one example). Because the honor of His Name is so important to Him (and should be to us as well), He *will* defend that Name by regathering Israel. There are many passages in Scripture which indicate God's displeasure with the way His Name has been dragged through the mud. It was the nation of Israel (the unbelieving Jews here) which created this intolerable situation, which required God to send judgment time and time again. Because other nations overcame them, they *assumed* Israel's God had become powerless.

• **No Form or Method** – when looking at the Bible from the viewpoint of Replacement Theology, it quickly becomes apparent that the views understood from Scripture are *read into* the text. This is nothing more than Eisegesis. On the other hand, the careful interpreter of God's Word approaches the Bible with the question, "What does it say?" instead of "What does it mean to me?" This is an important difference. The Bible should never be read into for meaning, but meaning should always be gained from it. Because of the Replacement Theologian's approach, anything that even remotely applies to Israel from the Old Testament is applied to the Church instead. Well-known verses spoken to Israel in the form of promises now become the Church's. This is only because the Replacement Theologian reads into Scripture by allegorizing, arriving at the meaning they wish to arrive at.

• **Difference Between the Testaments** – if one is to spiritualize or allegorize everything that applies to Israel in the Old Testament, making it applicable now exclusively to the Church, the actual connection is completely eradicated! In essence, Replacement

Theology denies the literal truth of Scripture, preferring instead an artificial truth that they impose on it. An artificial or man-made truth is no truth at all.

- **The New Testament** – if we were to substitute the word "Church" with every instance the writers used the word "Israel," it would not make sense. This can only be done when the interpreter allegorizes Scripture.

- **Israel Separate from the Church** – the New Testament makes it abundantly clear that the Church is continually separate from Israel. As Arnold Fruchtenbaum states, the Church has become *partakers* with Israel, not *over* takers (cf. Footsteps of the Messiah). This is a truth that few give heed to anymore. Too many within the Church believe that the Church has completely pushed Israel out of the picture entirely, with the Church having superseded and even become superior to Israel.

- **He Must Be a Liar** – because Replacement Theology *changes* what God has said, it is, in fact, guilty of making a liar out of God. When God promised that Israel would have the land forever, Replacement Theology states that the covenant to Abraham was *conditional.* Since Israel broke that covenant, then God is free from the obligation of fulfilling it. This of course would be true *if* – and *only if* – it can be proven that the covenant God made with Abraham was actually a conditional covenant. Numerous biblical scholars have easily shown that the covenant was and remains *unconditional* in nature. If it was unconditional in nature, we have no other choice but to say that God broke His promises (if we are to believe that the Church is now Israel). If He could break His promises to Israel, what is to stop Him from breaking promises to the Church, or to individual Christians?

13

God's Promises Will Prevail

It would seem, whether we like it or not, that God will fulfill the promises He has made. Whether we interpret them correctly or wrongly will affect how we see things, but will in no way affect the outcome of each and every one of God's promises.

Israel rose again against all odds in 1948. She not only survived numerous skirmishes with other nations, but God blessed Israel enough to decisively come out the winner in the Six-Day War of 1967. He did this *not* for Israel's sake, but for *His* sake – for *His* glory and for *His* honor.

The idea that God is not only finished with the nation of Israel but stands against her goes against the entirety of biblical truth. God is going to *use* Israel to bring glory and honor to His Name. He will make the world see who He is and He will accomplish this on the back of the nation of Israel, the very nation that brought dishonor to His marvelous Name in the first place.

The whole issue of God's faithfulness to Israel reminds me of the extra-biblical reasons people have for trying to prove that the PreTrib Rapture is false. These folks hold up comments or statements from people like Corrie Ten Boom or Ruth Graham as if those statements are biblically inspired. They're not. They are merely the opinions of *people*.

Some also comment that the reason PreTribbers are so is because they want to avoid persecution. It is an absurd claim, as if my wishing it could make it so. No amount of prayer or wishful thinking on my part would cause me to miss the Tribulation period and the tremendous amount of persecution that comes from it *if* that is what God has in store for me. It is as simple as that, and it is undeniable.

I can no more wish my future death away by "creating" some biblical doctrine that says I will never die than I can create a PreTrib Rapture by merely believing that it will occur. If the PreTrib Rapture is not taught in the Bible, it won't happen. It is that simple.

I firmly believe that with the current administration of the United States, under the leadership of Mr. Obama, this country is going into a huge downward spiral. This is not necessarily due to the immorality in this country, though that is part of the whole picture.

I believe the one thing that is causing this country to take the downward spiral it has taken (and will continue to take if nothing is done to stop it) is the fact that our administration is essentially *cursing* Israel. We have never really had a president who is this adamant about wanting Israel to be destroyed. Oh, he doesn't say it like that, but his "peace" process is really much more about peace for Arabs and Muslims in spite of Israel.

This current administration is standing dangerously opposed to God and what He *will* accomplish through Israel. God's promises to Abraham remain. He has never rescinded them.

Those who curse Israel, God will curse. Those who bless Israel, God will bless. As I search the Scriptures, I find no place where these promises were ever changed or rescinded. The only possible way to get to a point where the promises *change* is by allegorizing Scripture so that it says something that it does not mean.

If we consider our country today (and this book is being written in June of 2011), we see high unemployment, a debt ceiling that Mr. Obama wants raised higher than it currently is (instead of doing something to *reduce* our debt), and a spending spree in Washington, DC under Mr. Obama that will have him spending 3.2 Trillion dollars by the end of this year. Unfortunately, our Federal government only takes in 2.2 Trillion dollars annually.

A few years ago, the people voted and put Mr. Obama in office. His plan for America has always been to change its course. He has done that, and unfortunately, it has led to nothing good.

Jack Kelly (Grace Through Faith) wrote an article cataloging the incidents of natural disasters and how they may very well relate to the things our leaders have done, going all the way back to Bush Sr. Kelly's article is an eye-opener and offers insight into what God may, in fact, be saying about any attempts to divide up *His Land*. This is the overriding problem today. People do not see the Land of Israel as being God's Land.

While on one hand, God owns all that He has created, according to the Bible, the nation *and* the Land of Israel were both specifically created and set aside by Him for His purposes. Certain people have come along thinking they know far better than God does and believe that if the people of Israel and the Arabs will agree to divide up the Land as they suggest, then all will be well. Will it? According to Kelly, God may very well be sending us dire and repeated warnings that people need to leave *His Land* alone.

In his article called *Is God Judging Us?* Kelly invites us to consider the numerous natural disasters that have occurred since 1991 with President Bush, Sr. During that period, *"As President George H. W. Bush is opening the Madrid (Spain) Conference to consider 'land for peace' and Israel's Middle East role, the 'perfect storm' develops in the North Atlantic, creating the largest waves ever recorded in that region. The storm travels 1000 miles from 'east to west' instead of the normal 'west to east' pattern and crashes into the New England Coast. Thirty-five foot waves pound Kennebunkport, Maine, the summer home of the Bush family."*[40]

Some may look at events like this and consider them nothing more than coincidental. That's their choice, but to me, when I see them laid out as Kelley has laid them out, they seem much more than simply coincidental. Consider the following.

"2. August 23, 1992: Hurricane Andrew – When the Madrid Conference moves to Washington DC and the peace talks resume, Hurricane Andrew, the worst natural disaster ever to hit America, comes ashore and produces an estimated $30 billion in damage and leaving 180,000 homeless in Florida.

"3. January 16, 1994: Northridge Earthquake—President Bill Clinton meets with Syria's President Hafez el-Assad in Geneva. They talk about a peace agreement with Israel that includes giving up the Golan Heights. Within 24 hours, a powerful 6.9 earthquake rocks Southern

---

[40] http://gracethrufaith.com/ikvot-hamashiach/is-god-judging-us/ (accessed 6/6/2011)

California[.] This quake, centered in Northridge, becomes the second most destructive natural disaster to hit the United States, behind Hurricane Andrew.

"4. January 21, 1998: Lewinsky Scandal – Israeli Prime Minister Benjamin Netanyahu meets with President Clinton at the White House and is coldly received. Clinton and Secretary of State Madeleine Albright refuse to have lunch with him. Shortly afterwards on that day, the Monica Lewinsky scandal breaks into the mass media and begins to occupy a major portion of Clinton's time.

"5. September 28, 1998: Hurricane George – As Secretary of State Albright works on the final details of an agreement in which Israel would give up 13 percent of the West Bank, Hurricane George slams into the United States Gulf Coast with 110 mph winds and gusts up to 175 mph. The hurricane hits the coast and is stalled there. On September 28, Clinton meets with Yasser Arafat and Netanyahu at the White House to finalize this land deal. Later, Arafat addresses the United Nations about declaring an independent Palestinian state by May 1999, as Hurricane George pounds the Gulf Coast, causing $1 billion in damage. At the exact time that Arafat departs the country, the storm begins to dissipate.

"6. October 15-22, 1998: Texas Flooded – On October 15, 1998, Arafat and Netanyahu meet at the Wye River Plantation in Maryland. The talks are scheduled to last five days with the focus on Israel giving up the aforementioned 13 percent of the West Bank. The talks are extended and conclude on October 23. On October 17, awesome rains and tornadoes hit southern Texas. The San Antonio area is deluged with rain. The rain and flooding in Texas continue until October 22 and then subside. The floods ravage 25 percent of Texas and leave over one billion dollars in damage. On October 21, Clinton declares this section of Texas a major disaster area.

"7. November 30, 1998: Market Capitalization Evaporates – Arafat comes to Washington again to meet with President Clinton to raise money for a Palestinian state with Jerusalem as the capitol. A total of 42 other nations were represented in Washington. All the nations agreed to give Arafat $3 billion in aid. Clinton promised $400 million, and the European nations $1.7 billion. On the same day, the Dow Jones average drops 216 points, and on December 1, the European Market had its third worst day in history. Hundreds of billions of market capitalization were wiped out in the U.S. and Europe.

"8. December 12, 1998: Clinton is Impeached – As Clinton lands in the Palestinian-controlled section of Israel to discuss the 'land for peace' process, the House of Representatives votes four articles of impeachment against him.

"9. May 3, 1999: The Powerful Super Tornado – On the day that Yasser Arafat is scheduled to declare a Palestinian state with Jerusalem as the capital, the most powerful tornado storm system ever to hit the United States sweeps across Oklahoma and Kansas. The winds are clocked at 316 mph[,] the fastest wind speed ever recorded. The declaration is postponed to December 1999 at the request of President Clinton, whose letter to Arafat encourages him in his 'aspirations for his own land.' He also writes that the Palestinians have a right to 'determine their own future on their own land' and that they deserve to 'live free, today, tomorrow and forever.'

"10. Week of October 11, 1999: Hurricane, Earthquake and Dow Collapse – As Jewish settlers in 15 West Bank settlements are evicted from covenant land, the Dow-Jones financial averages lose 5.7 percent in the worst week since October 1989. On October 15 the Dow lost 266 points, and a hurricane slammed into North Carolina. On the next morning, October 16, a magnitude 7.1 earthquake rocked the southwest in the fifth most powerful earthquake in 20th Century. The earthquake was centered in the California desert and did little damage but was felt in three states. (source: www.truthorfiction.com)

"11. August 29, 2005. Hurricane Katrina. One week before Katrina made landfall, Israel carried out the evacuation of 9,500 residents from Gush Katif and four Samaria communities. Residents were forced from their homes by Israeli troops, some dragged away kicking and screaming and placed on buses that took them from the area. The Gaza evacuation had been supported and even urged upon Israel by the US. Estimated to have caused damages in excess of $100 billion Katrina was one of the most expensive natural disasters in US history (Source: www.wnd.com/news/article.asp?ARTICLE_ID=46178)

"12. Sept. 1, 2010 US Pres. Obama welcomed PM Netanyahu (Israel) Pres. Abbas (Palestinians) Pres. Mubarak (Egypt) and King Abdullah (Jordan) to the White House, having invited them all to dinner on the eve of the first direct negotiations between the Israelis and Palestinians in nearly two years. As the talks began, Hurricane Earl (a category 3 storm) was headed for North Carolina where mandatory evacuation orders were issued in some coastal areas. Hurricane warnings were established all the way up the East coast to Cape Cod. Although many experts felt the timing was wrong, and in fact no tangible results came from the talks, over $40 million in damages were attributed to hurricane Earl."[41]

As we can see, the tide has been turning against Israel for some time, and our leadership has been consistently sneaky about it in some cases. Mr. Obama is simply carrying on what his predecessors began and is attempting to go even further than they did. They set the tone and laid the groundwork, and he is carrying the baton.

Right now, the United States of America is in the crosshairs (a figure of speech) of God's scope. We are being judged and our economy, our debt, the natural disasters like flooding, tornadoes, earthquakes and more, are all proof of that.

---

[41] http://gracethrufaith.com/ikvot-hamashiach/is-god-judging-us/

In fact, what we see in the Obama Administration is a resolute desire to spend far more money than the government actually takes in each year. Just recently, Mr. Obama pledged financial support for Greece in the face of their economic crisis. Mr. Obama somehow tied the problems in Greece with problems in the United States, justifying his promises of help to Greece.

The problem, of course, is that Mr. Obama seems much more willing and able to help other countries than he does the United States. Mr. Obama has spent millions on projects in Afghanistan and Egypt as well as nearly one *billion* U.S. dollars in an attempt to rebuild the Gaza Strip.

Beyond this, one of Mr. Obama's favorite projects seems to be rebuilding mosques throughout the world, a program which began under Bill Clinton. However, at a time when our own country desperately needs financial solutions, should we continue rebuilding things in other parts of the world while people in this country are suffering?

Mr. Obama does this while cutting areas that should not be cut, in my opinion. This past January, Defense Secretary Robert Gates announced that the Pentagon would be cutting 78 million dollars from its budget over the next five years. This will obviously impact our military resources. By the way, these 78 million dollars is in *addition* to the 100 million dollars in cuts that Gates already stated would be cut from the Pentagon's budget, bringing the total to 178 *million* dollars. There will be a reduction of at least 10,000 marines and at least 27,000 in the army. So what is Mr. Obama doing? It would seem as though he is cutting back on the ability of this country to defend itself. I'm not sure how a person could arrive at an alternative conclusion.

One of the things Mr. Obama continues to do is play the blame game, passing off blame for current conditions on his predecessor, George

W. Bush. Not only is this not fair, but it is not true because Mr. Obama has been funding things that have far outspent his predecessor. The idea that Mr. Bush got this country to where it is now is 100% wrong and most people are waking up to that fact.

Since Mr. Obama's *first* year in office, he – all by himself – has *tripled* the national debt of the United States. During his second year in office, the deficit went to 1.29 *trillion* dollars. Under Obama, the debt continues to rise and now he wants Congress to raise the debt ceiling, presumably so that he can continue to put this country even further in debt.

The reality is that Mr. Obama simply outspends what our government takes in annually and he shows no sign of letting up on that spending. It is clear that he wants to destroy this country's very foundation and he cannot spend fast enough for his own tastes.

The only solution is to get back to the point where we support Israel and what God is going in and through them. To do otherwise is to invite His judgment and wrath. This is where we are *now*. We do not need to stay here.

God does not expect us to *agree* with the faults and failures and even the immorality of Israel. He expects us to support *His plan* for and through Israel. That's what He expects from us. We cannot condemn Israel and ignore the other countries surrounding it as if they are innocent, but most importantly, we should be supporting the notion that God has restored and will continue to restore Israel because a plan He has put in motion will come to full fruition. There is nothing we can do to stop it. The only thing we can do is invite trouble and judgment upon ourselves because we stand opposed to God's will regarding the nation and the Land of Israel.

14

What About You?

Do you know *when* you will die? Are you aware of the *day* and *hour* when you will slip from this life into eternity? I'm betting you are not privy to that information. So why are you living as if you **<u>do</u>** *know when it will happen?* Putting a decision about Jesus off until another day is taking a huge chance because of the fact that you do not know when you will die. That is plainly simple, and logic alone demands that you do not put this decision off. Yet you do, because the thought of becoming a Christian makes you feel uncomfortable.

You wrongly believe that to become a Christian means that you have to change in a major way *before* Jesus will accept you. It means to you giving up the things you love now because if you love them, then obviously they are wrong and God does not love them.

You are putting the cart before the horse. You must understand that God is not rejecting you. He is not standing there, tapping His foot, demanding that you eliminate those things that He does not like before you can come to Him for salvation.

If you (or anyone) could do that, you would not *need* His salvation at all. It is because you and I do things that are not pleasing to Him that we need His salvation.

What do you do that you would like to no longer do? Do you drink excessively until you cannot control it? Do you play around with drugs? Do you eat too much food until you have become overweight, lethargic and sickly?

What other things are in your life that you do not like? Are you drawn to illicit extra-marital affairs? Do you have a problem with lust? Are you a shopaholic? Do you tend to tell lies a great deal because it makes you feel important, or to hide things about your life?

Do you find that you do not like people and you would prefer to be around animals or out in the woods than around people? Are you a workaholic? Do you place a high value on money and you find that you work very hard to obtain it?

Here's the problem. The enemy of our souls comes to us and tells us that God will never accept us until we get rid of those things. He lies to us that God essentially wants us "perfect" before He will be willing to meet us and grant us eternal life. This is completely untrue.

The other lie that our enemy tells us is that we should not become a Christian because the fun in our life will fly out the door. We will no longer be able to drink or do the fun things we enjoy now. We start to think that coming to God means becoming a doormat for people and having to fill our life with things we do not want to *ever* do.

These are all lies, and unfortunately, too many people believe them. First of all, God does not expect you to be "perfect" before you come to Him for salvation. If that were the case, no one would be able to ever approach Him.

Secondly, God does not say that He is going to take away all the things we enjoy and replace them with things we hate. What is wrong with enjoying the lake on your boat? What is wrong with spending a day with the family fishing or just relaxing in the mountains? There is nothing wrong with these things.

What God *will* do is begin to remove the things that have ensnared you so that life is actually draining from you, but you are not aware of it. For instance, maybe you drink excessively and you have tried everything you can think of to quit. You have gone to AA meetings, spent thousands of dollars on this program or that, and you have even used your own will power to free yourself from the addiction to alcohol, all to no avail.

The question is not: *do I need to quit before I come to Jesus?* The question is: *am I willing to allow Him to work in and through me to take away the addiction I have to alcohol?* Do you see the difference? Are you willing to allow Him to work in you to break that addiction so that you will become a healthier person, one who is able to think straight and one who learns to rely on Him for strength? That is all He wants you to be able to do. He knows you cannot break that addiction (or any addiction for that matter) with your own strength and willpower. Are you willing to allow Him to do it in and through you?

What if you are a workaholic? What if you have "things" like a boat, a house in Cancun, a large bank account, four cars, and more? Do you think that God is going to ask you to give it up, or worse, do you think that God will simply come in and take all of that from you? I know of nothing in Scripture that tells us He will do that.

What God will do with all of those who come to Him trusting Him for salvation is one thing, which begins the moment we receive salvation and will continue until the day we stand before Him. He will begin to create within us the character of Jesus (cf. Ephesians 2:10).

Here is a verse from the Old Testament that was said originally through the prophet Ezekiel to the people of Israel. While this was specifically stated to the Jews, it is applicable to all who receive salvation through Jesus Christ.

"I will give you a new heart and put a new spirit within you; I will take the heart of stone out of your flesh and give you a heart of flesh. I will put My Spirit within you and cause you to walk in My statutes, and you will keep My judgments and do them" (Ezekiel 36:26-27).

God is speaking here through Ezekiel, and He is saying that He will give the people a new heart of flesh, removing that old heart of stone. This is God's responsibility. God is the One who makes that happen. We are told in the book of Hebrews that God is the Author and Finisher of our faith (cf. Hebrews 12:2). This tells me that God is the One who changes me from within so that over time, my desires are slowly turned into His desires.

I recall years ago thinking that God wanted to do everything in my life that I did not want Him to do. I fell into the asinine belief that He wanted to change everything about me. What I learned is that yes, there are things that God does want to change about me. However, there is a lot that God originally gave me that He has also enhanced and used for His glory.

Maybe you are a workaholic who thinks that working hard is something God does not want you to do. This is not necessarily the case. He may have given you the ability and the knowledge to work in the area of finance for a great purpose. All He may wind up doing is dialing back your workaholic tendencies so that you have more time to enjoy your family and study His Word.

But you say you smoke, or drink, or use illegal drugs, and you don't want to give those up. As I stated, you can't give those up under your own power, and the fact that you have tried so many times has proven it to you.

But God knows what is and what is not good for you. Are you willing to *allow* Him to work in you to change your desires so that you no longer want to smoke, use illegal drugs, or drink nearly as much?

Then you say that you believe God wants to make you a Christian so you can become miserable. Isn't that what most Christians are; miserable? Not the Christians I know, and certainly not me, my wife, or our children.

Where does the Bible say that God wants us miserable? You will not find it. What God wants is for us to be blessed, and that begins when we receive salvation from His hand.

You know, if we would stop and take the time to consider the fact that this life is exceedingly short if we compare it to eternity, we will then realize that there is nothing so important that it should keep us from receiving Jesus as Savior and Lord.

Unfortunately, too many people do not consider the brevity of life. They think they will live forever, or at the very least, they will die when they are really old and gray. That will come too soon. This author is going to be 54 years old in just a few months from this writing. It truly seems like yesterday that I was a young boy fishing in the Delaware River near Hobart, New York. There I spent many Saturdays fishing and simply enjoying being outdoors. How did life go by so very quickly? How could that have happened?

It has happened, and I am at a point in life where not only do I realize that this life is short, but I actually look forward to spending eternity with Jesus after this life. Does that sound morbid to you? It shouldn't, because by comparing this life to eternity, we should get a sense of what is truly important.

God does not expect us to become Mother Theresas. He does not necessarily expect us to give up everything and become missionaries in outer Mongolia. What God expects is for us to simply allow Him to change our character as He sees fit.

Over time, we may well find that we have simply stopped swearing without realizing it. Our desire for cigarettes or alcohol has nearly evaporated. Illicit affairs no longer enter the picture.

We also may find that some of the things we want to eliminate in our life become more pronounced. Often the enemy will do this to cause us to focus on something that God is not even doing in our lives at that point. It causes tension, frustration, and self-anger.

If you have gotten to this point in your life and you have not dealt with the question about Jesus, it is about time you do so. You need to stop what you are doing and realize a couple of things before you go through another minute in this life.

- **Sinner**: you need to realize that you are a sinner. You have sinned and you will continue to sin. Sin is breaking the laws that God has set up. We all sin. We have all broken God's laws and that breaks any connection we might have had with God. Sin pushes us away from Him.

    Romans 3:23 says *"For all have sinned, and come short of the glory of God."* That means you and that means me. All means all. That is the first step. We need to recognize and agree with God that yes, we are sinners. I'm a sinner. You are a sinner. This results in God's anger, what the Bible terms "wrath."

- **God's Wrath**: Romans 1:18 says, *"For the wrath of God is revealed from heaven against all ungodliness and unrighteousness of men, who suppress the truth in unrighteousness."*

This is as much a fact as the truth that we are all sinners. Because we are sinners – by breaking God's law(s) – God has every right to be angry with us and ultimately destroy that which is sinful. If we choose to remain "in" our sinful states throughout this life, we will – unfortunately – be destroyed with the rest of sin.

Fortunately, there *is* a remedy, and it is salvation.

- **God's Gift**: In the sixteenth chapter of Acts, a jailer asks Paul this famous question: *what must I do to be saved?* The question was asked because Paul and Barnabas had been imprisoned, and while there, they began singing praises to God.

God then sent a powerful earthquake that opened the doors to all the prison cells, yet no one escaped. When the jailer arrived, he saw that everyone was still in their cells, and after seeing that miracle (what prisoner would not want to escape from prison?), turned and asked what he must do to be saved. He was speaking of the spiritual aspect of things. He wanted to know how he could be guaranteed eternal life.

The answer Paul gave the man was, *"Believe on the Lord Jesus Christ, and thou shalt be saved, and thy house"* (Acts 16:31).

This is not head knowledge or intellectual assent. This is *believing from the heart.* In fact, Paul makes a very similar statement in another book he wrote, Romans. He says, *"That if thou shalt confess with thy mouth the Lord Jesus, and shalt believe in thine heart that God hath raised him from the dead, thou shalt be saved. For with the heart man believeth unto righteousness; and with the mouth confession is made unto salvation"* (Romans 10:9-10).

When we fully believe something, we confess that it is true. It must begin in the heart because that is where the will is located. We must want to believe. We must endeavor to believe. We must seek to believe.

We must stop giving ourselves all the reasons to deny or ignore Jesus. As God, He became a Man, born of a virgin. He clothed Himself with humanity that He might show us how to live, and in so doing, would keep every portion of the law.

If Jesus was capable of keeping every portion of the law, then He would be found worthy to become a sacrifice for our sin – yours and mine. If He became a sacrifice for our sin, then all that we must do is embrace Him and His sacrificial death.

In short then, to become saved we must:

1. Admit (we sin)
2. Repent (want to turn away from it)
3. Believe (that Jesus is the answer)
4. Embrace (the truth about Jesus)

We **admit** that we are sinner, that we have sinned. This is nothing more than agreeing with God that we have broken His law. Can you honestly say that you have not broken God's law? If you admit to breaking even the "smallest" law, then you are a lawbreaker.

After we admit that we have sinned, the next step is found in **repenting**. Some believe that repenting is actually moving away from sin. This author believes that it is a willingness to move away from sin, and there is a difference.

As we have already discussed, it is impossible to stop sinning. Human beings simply cannot do it because as long as we live, we will have a sin nature, which is something within us that gives us a propensity to sin. As long as we have this inner propensity to sin or break God's laws, we will never be perfect in this life.

We cannot one day say "Lord, I promise to stop sinning." If we do that, we are only kidding ourselves and setting ourselves up for major failure. We cannot stop sinning in this life. The most we can do is *want* to stop sinning and then spend the rest of our lives allowing God to create the character of Jesus within us, slowly, little by little.

Repenting is to decide that you no longer want to do the things that keep us out of heaven. We no longer wish to break God's laws. It is not promising God that we will never sin again.

Once we admit, then repent, we must **believe**. This is one of the most difficult things to do because believing that Jesus died in our place, that He lived a perfectly sinless life, is extremely difficult to believe. Our minds cannot grasp that truth. We must ask God to open our eyes to that truth so that we can embrace it.

While on the cross next to Jesus, the one thief joined the other thief in ridiculing Jesus. Then, all of a sudden – as we read in Luke 23 – this same thief that had just been ridiculing Him now turned to Him with a new understanding.

It was this new understanding that prompted the thief to say to Jesus, *"Lord, remember me when you come into your Kingdom."* Jesus looked at the man and responded to him, *"Today, you will be with me in paradise."*

What had occurred in the mind and heart of that thief from one moment to the next? One thing, and that one thing was that God opened the thief's eyes so that he could see the truth. It was as if the blinders fell off and he now saw and understood who Jesus was, even to the most cursory degree that Jesus was dying not for Himself, but for others.

It was this understanding, this awareness, which prompted the man to ask Jesus to simply be remembered. Jesus went way beyond it to promise the man that he would be with Jesus that day in paradise.

Please notice in Luke 23 that there is nothing in the chapter that tells us that the man promised Jesus he would give up sin, or that he would never sin again. There is nothing that tells us that thief took the time to enter into a final deathbed confession of his sins so that he could be absolved.

The thief made no promises to Jesus at all. What he experienced was the truth of who Jesus was and what Jesus accomplished for humanity. Jesus accomplished what we cannot. What is left is for each person to *admit*, *repent*, *believe*, and *embrace*.

Let me clarify here that though we do not see any verbal repentance from the thief, we know that he did repent. He admitted as well. How can we know this? Because of the thief's complete about-face with respect to his attitude toward Jesus. One minute, he was ridiculing Jesus, and the next, embracing Him. This is important. There is no way he could have or would have *embraced* Jesus had he not been humbled by the truth *about* Jesus.

Once the thief saw the truth, he was instantly humbled. Within himself, he knew that he was a sinner, and in fact the text states that this is what he told the other thief dying next to him. *"But the other answering rebuked him, saying, Dost not thou fear God, seeing thou art in the same condemnation? And we indeed justly; for we receive the due reward of our deeds: but this man hath done nothing amiss"* (Luke 23:40-41). Something happened within the heart of the one thief. In one moment, the thief went from harassing Jesus to recognizing his own sinfulness, and then ultimately, asking for grace, which was freely given to him.

Whether he said it or not, the thief went from haughtiness to humility in a very short space of time, and it was all because he saw the truth about Jesus. That truth helped him realize that he deserved his death and what would happen to him after death. He understood that Jesus did not deserve death.

From here, the thief fully embraced the truth about Jesus and was rewarded with eternal life because of it. He did not come off the cross to be water baptized. He did not list a long litany of offenses against God. He recognized the truth about Jesus, was humbled, and embraced that truth!

This is what each of us needs to do. We cannot give in to the lie that tells us that we are not good enough, or we have not given up enough before God will accept us. We must reject the lie that says we must somehow earn our salvation.

Jesus has done everything that is necessary to make salvation available to us. The only thing that is left for us is to see the truth. Once we see that truth, it should humble us to the point of embracing Jesus and all that He stands for and is to us.

The eighth chapter of Romans begins with the fact that all who trust Jesus for salvation are no longer condemned...*ever*. All of my sins –

past, present, and future – have not only been forgiven, but canceled. It is because of my faith in the atonement (death) of Jesus that God is able to cancel all of my sins, even the ones that I have not committed yet. This does not make me eager to commit them. It makes me want to do what I can to avoid sinning.

If you do not know Jesus, please do not put down this book without deliberately *believing* that He is God, that He died for you by the shedding of His blood on the cross, and that He rose three days later because death could not keep Him. Do you believe that? If you do not yet believe it, do you *want* to believe it? If so, then simply ask God to help you come to believe all that Jesus is and all that He has accomplished for you. God will answer your prayers and you may either receive instantaneous awareness of all that Jesus is and has done, or it may be a *growing* awareness over time. In either case, it is the most important decision you will ever make.

Turn to Him now and pray for knowledge of the truth and an ability to embrace it. Please. He is waiting for you.

Ask Yourself:

1. Do you *know* Jesus? Are you in *relationship* with Him? Have you had a spiritual transaction according to John 3?
2. Do you *want* to receive eternal life through the only salvation that is available?
3. Do you believe that Jesus is God the Son, who was born of a virgin, lived a sinless life, died a bloody and gruesome death to pay for your sin, was buried, and rose again on the third day? Do you *believe* this?
4. Do you *want* to *embrace* the truth from #3?
5. Pray that God will open your eyes and provide you with the faith to begin believing the truth about Jesus. Ask Him to help your faith embrace the truth, realizing that you are not good enough to save yourself and that your sin will keep you out of God's Kingdom without His salvation.

6. Pray as if your life depended upon it because *it does*!
7. If you have prayed to receive Jesus as Savior and Lord, please write to me. I want to send you some materials at *no charge or obligation*. Write to me at **fred_deruvo@hotmail.com** and sign up for our free bimonthly newsletter at **www.studygrowknow.com**

Visit our page on **OnePlace.com/ministries/study-grow-know** to hear our latest broadcasts as well as those that have been archived.

There is a chaos coming that is predicated upon the rise of Islam, Satanic Soldiers, aliens, and evil beyond measure. As an ideology, Islam masquerades as a religious light to the world, one that promises to usher in world peace; but at what cost? Through the use of political strategies, military might, and religious tenets, adherents of Islam work within various established governments to create special laws or exemptions for Muslims in the hope of eventually overthrowing that established government. Can it happen? IS it happening? Find out in *Evil Rising*. ($13.95; 184 pages, 978-0977424429)

We hear all the time how bad things are getting throughout the world. Do we chalk it all up to being the normal cycles that occur in life, or is something else going on behind the scenes? What if this generation alive now turns out to be the last one before Jesus returns? Is there any truth at all to the claim that Jesus will return one day? If you are one who has not taken the time to read through some of the books of the Bible that are said to teach truths regarding the last days, *Living in the Last Generation* puts it out there in a straightforward manner, making it easy to understand. ($11.95; 132 pages. ISBN: 978-0977424405)

www.ingramcontent.com/pod-product-compliance
Lightning Source LLC
Chambersburg PA
CBHW080438110426
42743CB00016B/3206